SERENITY GRIMOIRE

Manifest Happiness with Magick

David W. Cropper

ISBN: 979-8-9890530-6-3 (Hardcover)
ISBN: 979-8-9890530-7-0 (Paperback)
ISBN: 979-8-9890530-8-7 (Ebook)

Library of Congress Control Number:

CONTENTS

Not all books include dedications, but many authors choose to share a special thank you to someone(s) who have made an impact on the writing of the book. This may be on a personal or professional level and can range from heartfelt to comedic and anything in between.

Dedication text is traditionally center aligned.

NOTE FROM THE AUTHOR

Authors Note:

This book is a journey crafted to captivate its readers and lead them on an adventure of the soul. Its intention is not to challenge or negate anyone's religious or spiritual beliefs but rather to offer a new lens through which to view the world.

Within these pages lie unique spells born from the author's imagination and creativity. They stand alone as original creations; any similarities to those practiced by other magickal practitioners are purely coincidental.

While magick can be a potent tool for self-discovery and growth, it should never be relied upon as the sole means of progress. Practical action and sound decision-making must always come first.

It is imperative to understand that magick is not a substitute for professional guidance or medical advice. In times of need, always seek assistance from trained professionals.

And above all else, remember to approach magick cautiously and prioritize safety at all times.

CHAPTER ONE

CHAPTER 1: BOOK OF SPELLS

Have you ever wondered about the true essence of a grimoire? It is not merely a collection of spells, rituals, and enchantments but a sacred book imbued with generations of wisdom. Usually passed down through time, these written records contain the key to unlocking the secrets of the mystic arts.

Often referred to as a Book of Shadows, Spellbook, Codex, or Grimoire, the book is more than just a physical object. Within its pages lie the echoes of past conjurers, their energy and essence imprinted upon the very paper they have touched.

For those who create their own spellbooks, each stroke of ink or click of the keyboard holds immense power and signifies the culmination of their knowledge and abilities. A spellbook is not just a book, but a vessel for magick and wisdom."

Within the pages of this grimoire lie spells for the modern practicer, written to inspire and motivate even the most novice of magick spell casters. You do not need to be a Sorcerer, Witch, Warlock, or Wizard. The spells within these pages will empower you and transform your perception of the world around you.

This book of spells will serve as a guide for those with honorable intentions seeking to harness the true essence of magick and inner strength. It should unlock your dormant potential and foster a connection with the elements of Earth, Wind, Fire, Water, and Spirit. The words seem to pulse with energy and beckon the reader into a world of endless possibilities.

As you turn each page of this grimoire, open your mind and heart to the words of each spell. Some are simple incantations for protection, others to be used to call on the elements to assist with health and wealth, to open your third eye, along with many other spells to make you and those around you happy and sound. With an open mind and a strong will, each spell may unlock the hidden potential within yourself if you choose to heed its call.

What truly sets a grimoire apart from any other book? It is not just the carefully crafted words meticulously inscribed upon its aged pages. Nor is it solely the rituals and spells that lie within its bindings.

The true power of a grimoire lies in its ability to transport the reader to another realm, one where their mind will be opened to the universe around them, opening their eyes to what was unseen before. With each turn of the page, the mind is opened to a new spiritual world.

We will explore the rituals and spells that will enhance your life and well-being, teaching you how to harness the energy of the five elements mentioned to enhance your magical abilities. Everyone has the ability within them to harness the powers of the supernatural. From communicating with the spirits to creating spells, this book will guide you on a journey of self-discovery and connection to the natural and supernatural worlds.

So, seeker of knowledge and magick, are you ready to delve into the pages of the Serenity Grimoire and unlock the power within? Once you do and find your mind and spirit opened to magick, there is no going back.

With all witchcraft, it is neither good nor bad, right nor wrong. Casting spells is not inherently evil; it is all about why you cast them and what end you seek. Your own intentions will dictate the purity of the spellwork. Do as you will, but bring harm to none. Blessed Be. Now, let us begin our journey into the mystical realm of the magick.

The first thing that may jump out to you is the spelling of magick. You may be used to the word magic and maybe seeing the word magick for the first time. These two words have different meanings.

Magic: This term typically refers to stage magic, illusions, tricks, or entertainment designed to create a sense of wonder or mystery. It's the kind of magic you might see performed by a magician on stage or in a circus. In fantasy literature and popular culture, "magic" often refers to supernatural abilities or powers wielded by characters, often for various purposes like combat, healing, or transformation.

Magick: This term, often spelled with a "k" at the end, is commonly associated with occult practices, particularly within the traditions of ceremonial magick, spiritual philosophy, and various forms of witchcraft. In this context, "magick" is believed to be a method of harnessing and manipulating natural or divine forces to affect change in accordance with the practitioner's will. Adding the "k" is sometimes used to distinguish this concept from stage magic and indicate a more intentional, ritualistic practice.

The art of magick is as varied and unique as its many practitioners. It encompasses a vast array of traditions, beliefs, and techniques, from the elaborate ceremonial rituals of high magick to the simple folk practices handed down through generations.

What unites these diverse approaches is the underlying belief in the inherent power of the individual to manifest change in the world through deliberate intention and spiritual connection.

Each practitioner holds within themselves a deep understanding of their own personal power and the boundless potential that comes with it. For those who fully embrace this ancient craft, there are no limits to what can be achieved through the delicate balance of mind, body, and spirit.

Within the pages of this grimoire, we will be delving into the realm of "magick," that hidden force that fuels the practice of manifestation with spell casting. As you embark on your journey, you will come to comprehend the true essence and boundless potential of magick.

So, are you prepared to unlock the secrets of your mind and spirit? If so, let us begin our voyage into spell work to live a fulfilled life.

Each chapter is designated by a title that denotes the spells we shall undertake; detailed explanations of their purpose will precede the spells themselves. Together, we shall un-cover the power and wonder of magick.

As a practitioner of magick, it is crucial for one to center their focus and channel their energies towards achieving their ultimate goal. So heed this call, dear reader, and let the spells and the general life advice contained within Forest Grimoire be your guiding light as you delve into the world of magick.

Let the words inscribed on these pages become your sword, infusing you with the power to pierce through the shadows of your soul and reveal your true potential. With just a drop of determination and a hint of faith, you can embark on a journey into the supernatural that will forever change your path.

Along with this book, you will need a mirror and a few candles—the colors don't matter. Incense and/or sage are also helpful. Salt is also a powerful tool of protection. White noise music or sounds of nature can help you move along in your meditation and center your mind. Creating an altar can also be beneficial as it will act as a way to center your energy and honor your ancestors and spirit guides.

To assemble an altar, carefully select a safe and quiet space to serve as its home. This could be a secluded corner of a room adorned with offerings to a deity or just to the universe as a whole. It is best to choose a location where you can engage in your rituals without interruption, free from the distractions of the outside world. A tranquil oasis where you can connect with your higher power.

As you prepare to create your altar, it is important to cleanse the space first. This can be done by burning sage, sprinkling blessed water, or even using visualization to surround the area with a bright white light, purging any lingering negative energies.

By cleansing the space, you are creating a pure and welcoming environment for your spiritual work to take place.

Just as a master painter prepares their canvas before beginning their masterpiece, so too must you prepare your altar for the magick and intention you will infuse into it.

First, decide what items you want to display on your altar. These could include representations of the five elements: earth, air, fire, water, and spirit. For instance, a candle for fire, a bowl of water, a feather for air, and a small dish of salt or crystals for the earth. You may also want to include a photo of a loved one who has passed to represent the spirit and honor your ancestors.

Additionally, you can choose to incorporate deities or spiritual figures that hold meaning for you. This could be in the form of statues, pictures, or symbols. Some people also like to include symbols of their intentions – items representing their goals and desires, such as crystals, herbs, flowers, or written affirmations.

Remember that having an altar is a personal choice and part of your individual journey. There is no right or wrong way to practice Magick; it is up to you to determine what feels right. Just remember the principle, "Do as you will and bring harm to none." I celebrate your decision to open your mind and explore new ways of connecting with and utilizing spell casting in your life. Let us begin. Fasten your seat belt.

CHAPTER 2: OPEN YOUR MIND

To harness the power of magick, one must first find one's center and open one's mind to the spiritual world. This can be a challenging task. It is best to seek out a quiet and safe location where one can slip away from the distractions of the physical world and allow one's thoughts to wander freely, just as one would in meditation.

Before beginning, ensure that your chosen place is purified and spiritually cleansed. You can accomplish this by burning a bundle of sage, sending out a heartfelt prayer to the deity you feel most connected with, or visualizing a brilliant white light enveloping and protecting the space.

If you utilize an altar, be certain to have objects symbolizing the five elements—earth, fire, water, air, and spirit—in addition to a lit candle and a reflective mirror.

As you retreat to your safe place, imagine a white light acting as a barrier surrounding you. This invisible shield acts as a powerful defense against any lingering spirits or dark forces that may try to harm you.

Many skilled magick practitioners use pure white salt to create a sacred circle of protection around themselves, tapping into its purifying properties and symbolism. Within this guarded space, you can let go of any fears and focus on your intentions with complete peace of mind.

Salt has long been used to purify and cleanse physical spaces, objects, and individuals. Many cultures and religions believe it wards off evil spirits and negative energies.

Listening to soothing music or gentle white noise can also aid in relieving stress and allowing the mind to relax from negative thoughts and feelings. These are just a few recommendations as we delve into the enchantments that open our minds and hearts.

Our journey begins with the following spells. Do not fear or hesitate, dear reader. A strong will and faith in the spiritual realm will bring great success in your practice of magick and lead to a more fulfilled life.

First, create a sacred space by cleansing the area with sage, incense, visualization, or any other method you choose. Sit comfortably before your altar or designated quiet space, and place a candle before you. Light the candle and take several deep breaths to center yourself. Close your eyes and imagine a bright white light surrounding you, filled with positive energy to protect and guide you on your spiritual journey.

Recite the following words:

"Spirits in the light, ancestors of my blood, Open this servant's mind, let it be unclosed, and grant me a second sight to look upon the other realm. Guide me through the veil of the living and dead, from day into night. I ask and implore you to open my mind to the world unseen. So let it be."

Imagine a serene tranquility surrounding you, almost like a soft mist enveloping you. Allow yourself to feel the energy around you fully. Be receptive to any feelings or insights that may come to you; they could be as subtle as a faint breeze or as noticeable as a tingle on your skin. Listen for the voices of your spirit guides.

Take a deep, steady breath, open your eyes, and blow out the candle when you feel ready. Show gratitude to the spirits for their guidance. Always remember that your intent and belief are the key components of any spell. They serve as the foundation of your magick. Trust in yourself and the process, and you will expand your mind to connect with the spiritual realm.

Here is another spell that may help open your mind and connect you with the energies around you. Set up your altar or sacred space as before. Light a white candle and place it in front of you. Take a few deep breaths to ground yourself and release any tension in your body.

Repeat the following incantation:

"Air, fire, water, earth, and spirit intertwine. Bring forth knowledge and wisdom, and help open my mind. Spirit guides and ancestors, hear my call, Open my mind to the mystical world, and let me see beyond the wall. Let my third eye open, let me see with pure sight, Bring forth the secrets that remain out of sight."

Sit quietly and let the words' energy sink in. Visualize your mind opening, allowing you to be accessible to what is beyond the physical world. When you feel ready, blow out the candle and thank the elements and spirits for their aid and guidance.

Do not be discouraged if you do not immediately see visions or receive messages. Opening your mind to the spiritual world takes time and practice. Trust in the process and keep exploring and learning.

Beyond spell casting to connect with the spiritual world, you may also use meditation and journaling practices to help tap into the spiritual world. A clear mind free of all earthly distractions will be needed for your spells to take hold.

Magick is not just the mere utterance of spells or performance of rituals; it is faith and belief in a spiritual realm and a connection to the natural and supernatural worlds that coexist around us.

To truly experience the power of magick, you must open yourself up to the world seen and unseen around you. It is present in even the smallest of things – the crunch of leaves beneath our feet, the breeze brushing against our skin, and the refreshing sensation of raindrops falling. Magick permeates every aspect of our existence.

To begin your practice, try meditating or taking walks in nature. These activities can help you tap into the energies surrounding you. Simply observing birds, leaves, animals in motion, and the wind can aid in strengthening your connection to the spiritual world around you and within yourself.

Approaching the path of magick with an open mind and heart will make the journey clearer with each step. This grimoire contains spells that can empower and guide you with the basic practice of magick, hoping to provide a source of inspiration for your journey.

As you begin your journey into the world of magick, remember that it takes patience and persistence to master its secrets. Each step, whether it's communing with your spirit guides, casting spells, or simply observing the world with heightened awareness, brings you closer to understanding the people in your life and fulfilling your purpose on this earth.

Keep in mind that magic is a deeply personal practice, and what works for one person may not work for another. Trust your intuition and allow yourself the freedom to experiment with different techniques and traditions until you find what resonates with your soul. Don't be afraid to create your own spells and rituals along the way.

A mind closed off to different ideas is like a fortress, fortified and impenetrable. It stands tall and strong, shielding you from the outside world. But within its walls, there is safety at the cost of isolation and ignorance. The key to unlocking this door lies in opening yourself up to new perspectives and possibilities. Without this key, growth and true happiness will become unattainable.

The following spell is most potent when performed in close proximity to the person you wish to help awaken to the world around them. Take a piece of paper and write the spell on it. Place the paper on top of a photograph of your intended recipient, focusing your thoughts and intentions on your intentions.

Do not utter the words of this spell out loud, but instead repeat them silently in your mind with conviction. Your intentions must be pure and aimed at bringing only positivity into their lives; always remember to harm none in your pursuit of magick.

With each repetition, visualize the barrier surrounding their mind dissipating, allowing them to see all that they have been choosing to ignore. As you finish the final repetition, envision their eyes opening wide as if seeing the world for the first time, guided by the spirits themselves.

"Closed mind be no more. See what you choose not to see. (person's name), you will no longer be blind. The spirits have opened your eyes."

With this spell, we empower ourselves to navigate the realms of magick and extend our reach into the hearts and minds of others, fostering understanding and empathy.

Let it be a constant reminder that our journey in the mystical realm is not one we take alone; rather, it is intertwined with the lives of those around us, shaping the very fabric of our world with each word we speak or with each action we do, good or bad. As we close this chapter and turn to new adventures, may our minds remain open to all possibilities, our hearts overflowing with compassion, and our spirits ever eager to delve deeper into the mysteries of the unseen. Let us continue on this path with wonder and curiosity, knowing that every step we take has the power to shape and transform our reality.

CHAPTER THREE

CHAPTER 3: GOOD FORTUNE

C rafting magick spells for good fortune involves tapping into the purest form of intentions for abundance and prosperity for others and yourself. It requires opening yourself to the flow of the universe and connecting with the natural and supernatural forces of the world around you. To receive, you must also give. It is a delicate dance. It may be hard to believe, but the more we give, the more we will receive.

The pursuit of abundance should not be driven by selfish desires for personal gain but rather by a selfless mindset. It is not about accumulating wealth and possessions for oneself but about utilizing that abundance to give back to those in need within our community. True abundance is found in the act of sharing and giving freely rather than hoarding our resources. As I have long believed, the energy we put into the world will inevitably return to us, as karma plays its role in shaping our lives. Let us embody this principle and create a ripple effect of generosity and positivity.

Set your intentions and define what you wish to manifest. It could be the success of your business, a specific opportunity that you've been hoping for, or just a stroke of good luck. Paint a vivid picture of your desired outcome and say why you yearn for it out loud. Visualize every detail and let your intentions be known to the universe.

Here's a guide to help you write your own spells. Remember that these are just guidelines; you can adapt them to fit your beliefs and practices.

1. Prepare your sacred space or altar and center yourself through meditation or the best method for you.

2. Write your intentions on a piece of paper. Be specific and positive in your wording. State what you want as if you already have it.

3. Light a candle and focus on your intention, visualizing it as if you already have it. Repeat your intention aloud or in your mind slowly and with intention.

4. Burn the paper with your intentions written on it, releasing the energy into the universe. Be careful and mindful when burning the paper.

5. Thank the elements and spirits for their aid and guidance.

7. Close your ritual by extinguishing the candle. Remember, the power lies within you and your intention. Trust in the process and good fortune will come your way.

To attract financial prosperity, light a candle and visualize abundance flowing in your life, allowing you to give freely to others.

Repeat the following spell seven times:

"I am thankful for the Wealth and riches I have and for the opportunity to share them with those in need. Financial prosperity has become my destiny."

Here are some additional spells you may find helpful. However, do not be afraid to use them as a template to write your own, which may be more specific to your needs.

Light a candle and repeat the following chant three times:

"Opportunities abound and flow through me. Smooth paths and open doors of success are what I see."

To bring general good luck, light a candle while holding this written spell in your hand, visualize your life filled with good fortune, and repeat the following chant three times:

"I give thanks to the spirits who are my guides for the good luck that flows through my soul, which I share with those around me."

There are moments in our lives when we find ourselves in need and must seek aid and assistance from the unseen forces around us. In these times, we can turn to spellwork and harness the power of magick to benefit ourselves directly. However, we must be cautious when using this type of magick, for every action we take has consequences that ripple outward and affect those around us.

It is impossible to obtain something without indirectly involving others. To avoid causing harm to others with our desires and intentions, here is a spell that can limit asking for selfish requests. Stand before a mirror for this spell, gazing into your own reflection as you speak these words with conviction:

"I call upon the elements of earth, wind, fire, water, and spirit to aid me in releasing this hindrance from my path.

With a clear mind and unwavering will, I am empowered and protected, and I shall overcome all obstacles."

As you recite these words, envision the elements swirling around you, providing strength and protection as you release the obstacle standing in your way.

As you delve into the world of spells and magick, remember that success lies in setting your intentions with clarity and conviction. Believe in the potent power of your spells, and never doubt yourself or your abilities. With each incantation, channel your energy towards positive outcomes, manifesting your desires into tangible reality. Keep your heart pure, and let the forces of the elements guide you towards the path of light and goodness.

To manifest financial prosperity in your life, light a candle and envision cascading abundance flowing into your life, granting you the freedom to give to others generously. Speak aloud the following spell:

"I invoke the spirits that envelop me, guide me along my path towards success, grant me the vision to see what is unseen, and aid me in making wise decisions in my daily endeavors."

Watch the flickering flame dance and sway as if responding to your call, filling the room with an uplifting warmth and radiance. As you speak these words, feel the energy of your desires pulsating through every fiber of your being, attracting all that you desire. Embrace the power of this spell and trust that it will lead you towards a fulfilled and prosperous life.

With a single breath, extinguish the small flame of the candle as you settle into stillness and allow your mind to wander to your ambitions.

Envisioning your future path. Visualize each step of your goals, letting the spell take hold and guide you toward your success.

Good fortune magick may also be used to bless others in your life. Blessing another is the best way to receive blessings from the universe. To work a spell of fortune for another, take a picture of them and place it on your altar. If you do not have an altar, go to the woods and sit under a large tree, placing the photo in front of you. Say the person's name three times and then recite these words,

"With love in my heart, I cast this spell. May fortune and blessings upon [name of person] dwell. Luck, prosperity, and happiness anew. With all my faith, I ask, may their dreams come true."

The art of magick is a powerful tool, capable of unlocking a path of good fortune for yourself and your loved ones. But like any journey, it requires preparation and readiness to receive its blessings fully. Just as a traveler must be physically and mentally prepared for their journey, so too must one be on the road to prosperity in order for the magic to truly take effect. Like a key fitting perfectly into a lock, the alignment of mind, body, and spirit is essential for harnessing the true power of magick. Only then can its blessings flow freely and abundantly.

As you embark on this journey, take moments to pause and reflect on the spells you have performed. Notice your life's subtle but powerful shifts, and remain open to unexpected opportunities and blessings. With an open mind and a heart filled with pure intentions, you will witness the true magick unfold before you.

Let the Serenity Grimoire be your trusted guide, inspiring and empowering you as you delve deeper into the world of magick. May good fortune always find its way into your life through the pages of this book.

And now, dear seeker of magick, let us continue on towards a better life through the power of spell casting. Remember, good fortune comes through hard work and generosity, and spellcasting is just one branch of the tree of life.

Let your mind and heart remain open as we turn the pages ahead, for you never know what wonders and challenges await you. And if at any point you feel trapped in the maze of your own thoughts, do not hesitate to retrace your steps and revisit these past pages for guidance to open your mind again. Life can be a tumultuous journey, but with the assistance of open-mind spells, we have the power to break free from our mental prisons and continue on our path toward a truly fulfilling existence.

CHAPTER FOUR

CHAPTER 4: PROTECTION

A common tool in the arsenal of magick users, protection spells are vital for fending off harm and shielding against negative energies or malicious hexes from other spellcasters. These spells help form a barrier of defense, safeguarding both body and mind from potential threats, known and unknown, physical and spiritual.

When used with practical safeguards, these spells will act as a shield against most forms of danger, providing an impenetrable layer of protection for the practitioner.

These incantations are to serve as a type of psychic safeguard, forming a barrier of positive energy to repel negative forces. Here are several spells to safeguard yourself and your loved ones from harm. Keep in mind that the key to these spells is to concentrate your intention and channel your energy towards the desired outcome of protection.

To protect against general harm, cast this spell outdoors on a night during a full moon.

Use your finger to etch a circle into the ground and imagine a white shield enveloping you and those you care for. Set a lit candle in the middle of the circle and concentrate on its flickering light while chanting as if singing the following spell:

"I Evoke the power of the circle of life; Guardian ancestors and spirits guides, hear my voice. Keep us safe and free from all harm. Let no negative energy come to me or those I hold dear. Causing harm to none, so let it be."

As you feel the spell's energy enveloping and guarding you, take a moment to center yourself with deep breaths. When you feel safe, blow out the candle and express gratitude out loud to the spirits for their assistance from the spirit realm.

To create a protective shield, recite this spell at the strike of midnight. Sit in a comfortable, quiet place, slowly inhale and exhale, allowing your heart rate to lower. Imagine a bright white light enveloping you as you speak these words:

"As the night is dark as the day is light, Enlighten and protect me as I go on my way. All harm against me shall not penetrate this barrier. Protection now, I pray. Let my body, mind, and spirit be safe from all harm."

The spells mentioned above are not a foolproof guarantee of complete safety but rather a tool to decrease the impact of harm in your life. It is vital to utilize all available means of protection, be it practical or Mystikal, in order to maintain your well-being and security.

Always keep in mind that prevention is key, and it is your responsibility to take all necessary precautions to ensure your safety and good health.

Whether through physical measures or spiritual practices, do everything in your power to stay safe and protected from any potential dangers lurking in the world around you.

Protection spells come in various forms and can be cast in numerous ways. Magick practitioners often use a personal barrier or shield spell for daily protection. The main purpose of this spell is to safeguard the mind and body from negative energies that may be encountered throughout the day.

Many people in our world possess the ability to feel the emotions of others, known as empaths. But even those without this gift can still be swayed by the powerful emotional energies that emanate from those in their presence, whether it be uplifting or detrimental. Our surroundings and interactions constantly shift and influence our inner state, for better or worse.

Think of the person standing behind you in the service line at a coffee shop, and the barista is new and slow at their job, which is causing the person behind you to get upset because they are running late for work. Even though this person does not say anything, you can feel the negative vibe penetrating from them.

This, in turn, can cause you to feel anxious or agitated.

Think of when the day started your day, and it was filled with joy and vitality. The sun was shining, birds chirping, and the world felt alive. But then you encountered someone else's dark, negative energy, and your own mood began to shift. It was like a heavy cloud had descended upon you, weighing down your spirits and dampening your enthusiasm.

This is when a personal protection barrier could have been useful – a shield to block out the negativity and protect your own well-being. With this barrier in place, you could continue on with your day, unburdened by the weight of someone else's emotions.

Let's create a protective barrier that we can use daily to safeguard our happiness from the emotional baggage of others. As you get ready in the morning, gaze into the mirror and recite these words:

"As I look beyond my reflection, I see only joy and positivity coming my way today. Shield me from any negative energies that may cross my path. Let nothing harm me, and let me continue on with a happy spirit."

Embrace this spell with all your heart and soul, banishing any doubts or fears that may try to creep in, for today, joy shall be your constant companion. Let the warmth of positivity fill you up like a cup overflowing, and let it guide you through each moment of the day.

Trust in the magick and believe with unwavering faith, for it will surely bring about an abundance of happiness surrounding you like a golden aura, knowing that nothing can dim the radiance of your spirit.

When it comes to casting a protection spell, the effects go far beyond just creating a personal shield. The powerful forces of magick can also safeguard one's home or workplace from outside threats. However, it's important to remember that basic methods of protection should always be used in conjunction with magick – things like locking doors and windows, having a security system, or even having a dog or weapon for added defense.

A protection spell should not be seen as a quick and easy solution; rather, it should be viewed as an additional layer of security for the safety and well-being of your family and property.

Pure white salt can be a valuable tool for safeguarding your home. It's known for its ability to ward off negative energies and spirits. By sprinkling a line of salt across doorways and window sills, you can create a barrier that keeps out unwanted guests and deflects any hexes that may have been placed upon you.

As you sprinkle the salt, recite this protection spell:

"I call on the elements of earth, fire, air, water, and spirit. Protect this place from all harm. Let this barrier shield all who are welcomed within. May any harmful hexes be reflected back onto their caster."

As you carefully lay down the salt at the bottom of all openings into the space, focus your mind on a pure white light that will surround and shield you. Choose wisely who you invite into this sacred space, for once they are welcomed in, their energy can no longer be blocked. It is crucial only to allow those with positive intentions to enter within these boundaries. Trust in the power of this spell and know that you are creating a safe haven for yourself and those you hold dear.

Remember, as you learn and master protection spells, always using them with pure intentions is vital. The purpose is to safeguard yourself and others from harm, not to cause harm to anyone else. Allow these spells to aid you in creating a protective shield around yourself and those close to you, enabling you to move through life confidently and without fear.

Practitioners of magick often feel responsible not just for their own protection but also for safeguarding those they care about, even when distance separates them.

Through the power of protection magick, one can extend a protective barrier to loved ones who are far away. To perform such a spell, create a circle of salt on your altar or perform the ritual in the forest under a large, grounding tree if an altar is unavailable. Light a candle at the center of the circle and place photos of those you wish to protect within it. Speak their names aloud, focusing your intention on their safety, and speak the following spell three times:

"By the power of my spirit guides and the blood of my blood long gone, I call on you to provide a guiding light, bless, and protect those I love from all harm. So let it be."

To conclude the spell, again speak the names of your loved ones within the salt circle. Express gratitude to the spirits for their protection. Remember, performing these spells with pure intentions is essential, aiming to create a shield of safety and positivity around yourself and those you hold dear. Trust in the potency of these protective spells and embrace the confidence they bring, knowing that you and your loved ones are guarded against harm. Blessed Be.

CHAPTER FIVE

CHAPTER 5: HOUSE & HOME

Safeguarding one's home with the powerful forces of magick is an essential first step in creating a harmonious and fulfilling life. Whether you reside in a rented or owned space, your living quarters hold significant importance as your sanctuary. Having already mastered the art of protection spells, it is now time to explore spells for a peaceful home and for finding and acquiring your dream house. With these magickal tools at your disposal, you can manifest a safe and serene haven that nourishes your soul and brings joy to your life.

As the saying goes, 'home is where the heart is', and in truth, the truest sense of belonging and comfort can be found in our emotional connections and affections rather than the mere physical structure or geographic location of where we reside. It's not the four walls and roof that make a home, but the people inside and the memories created within its walls.

Home is a feeling, an intangible concept that cannot be defined by bricks and mortar alone. It's the warmth of a hug, the laughter shared around a table, and the love that fills every corner with its gentle embrace. No matter where we go in life, our true home always resides within our hearts.

As grown-ups living in the United States, we have the freedom to choose our living arrangements and who we live with unless we're in prison. But even then, it could be argued that our actions and decisions led us there.

As we embark on this chapter, let's begin by seeking out a place to call our own home if we do not already have one. While renting can be a viable option, I strongly believe that owning a house provides a sturdy foundation for us to flourish and strive toward achieving financial independence. Furthermore, our own home allows us to establish roots and cultivate a flourishing tree of life.

Crafting a stable financial plan is an absolute necessity when it comes to the daunting task of purchasing a house. This endeavor demands discipline in living within one's means, conscientiously setting aside funds for future use, and wisely investing any surplus income. Merely relying on magickal spells will not miraculously resolve financial troubles if one continuously spends beyond one's means, leaving nothing left over from one's earnings to build for the future.

If you find yourself caught in this precarious situation of bad money management, it is crucial to confront and tackle your irresponsible financial habits before even considering purchasing a home. Without a solid financial foundation, the dream of becoming a homeowner may seem like a distant mirage, just out of arm's reach.

It's like attempting to build a house on quicksand – no matter how beautiful the structure appears, it will inevitably crumble without a strong and sturdy base. So take the time to mend and fortify your finances, and then watch as the possibility of owning your own home becomes more concrete and within your grasp.

Magick can only help. Being practical with your money is the first step. After completing the practical steps, you can start manifesting spells. Find a safe and quiet place to meditate on your dream home. Allow yourself to imagine every detail, from the layout to the decorations. Negative thoughts may arise, but do not focus on them; instead, push them away.

Once you have a clear vision of your ideal home, don't immediately dismiss it with thoughts of "I can't afford it." Open your mind and ask yourself, "How can I afford this home?" Having the right mindset is crucial for achieving homeownership.

With a positive and determined mindset and a carefully constructed budget in hand, obtain a copy of your credit report from a reputable service such as Credit Karma or go to the three major credit bureaus directly. Experion, Trans Union, and Equifax. This invaluable tool will provide you with a comprehensive overview of your current debt and overall credit score, equipping you to create a strategic plan for paying off any outstanding balances and rectifying any potential discrepancies on your credit report.

Take a moment to write down all the debt you currently owe on a piece of paper. Light a candle and envision your dream house while burning the paper, reciting these words:

"Flickering flame of desire, rid me of this financial burden. Grant me the wisdom to budget wisely and save diligently to manifest my ideal home."

Perform this spell weekly, but remember that wise financial choices are just as important as magick. This may require making changes, such as finding a new job or taking on additional side hustles.

The second crucial step in finding a safe and affordable home is enlisting the help of a reputable and compatible real estate agent. It's important to find someone who understands your needs, exudes positive energy, and possesses the necessary skills to negotiate a favorable deal on your behalf. As you embark on your home search, maintaining a mindset of optimism and setting clear intentions will guide you toward success in finding your dream home.

The following spell will assist you on your hunt for the perfect house. Recite the words twice daily while on your home search journey:

"So I seek, so I shall find, the house that is meant to be mine. Guardians of the Tree of Life aid my search for shelter anew."

If you are a homeowner looking to sell your property quickly, there are some helpful spells that can assist you on your journey to move on from your current house. Begin by cleansing your home of any residual negative energy that may be hindering the sale process.

Burn sage in every room, letting the fragrant smoke waft through the air and penetrate every nook and cranny of the house. Visualize the cleansing smoke sweeping away any lingering negativity or stagnant energy, leaving behind a purifying and rejuvenating atmosphere.

This will create a clean and welcoming space for potential buyers to envision themselves living in.

Then, write down the asking price and your desired profit on a piece of paper and light a candle. As the candle burns, visualize your house being sold quickly and for your desired price. Say these words,

"With this flame, I ignite the spark in the buyer's heart. May my home sell quickly and at the right price. A new chapter in my life I begin, so let it be."

As the candle burns down, continue to focus on your intention and trust that the universe will manifest your desired outcome. In addition to magick, ensure you have done all the necessary updates and repairs to your home to make it more attractive to potential buyers. And remember, the right buyer will come along at the right time; trust in the process and keep your energy positive.

Some of you may have heard that burying a miniature Saint Joseph statue upside down at the edge of your property can also help you sell your home. I, for one, will not advise you one way or the other about using this method in conjunction with magick, as many will see it as dealing with another form of religion with which they are not affiliated.

As an experienced and versatile real estate agent, I am always open to exploring different house–selling approaches. My resourcefulness and determination drive me to exhaust every possible avenue to swiftly and successfully sell a home for my clients. Whether it be through traditional methods or innovative magick techniques, making sure my clients are cared for matters more to me than someone's theology.

Living in a peaceful and harmonious home is essential for a happy and healthy life.

Making the right decisions about where and with whom to live is very important. If you live with another person or even a pet, there will be times of frustration, disagreements, and strife. Here is a spell to assist you when tension in the home is high.

"Flame of Life, let all frustrations cease, so there will be peace among those who live in this house. Help us find common ground so harmony and happiness can be found."

Envision a cozy and inviting home where affection and compassion are at the heart of every encounter. Take a moment to relax and allow this spell to bring calmness and tranquility to your household.

Sense any conflicts or arguments melting away, replaced by a feeling of harmony and empathy among all who reside there. Let the soothing rays of optimism and serenity spread throughout your home, establishing a sanctuary of love and consideration for all who cross its threshold.

CHAPTER 6: GOOD HEALTH

The practice of health magick is centered around using spells to promote holistic wellness. Whether it be for physical, mental, or emotional ailments, this approach aims to restore balance and harmony within the body and mind. Various traditions surrounding health magick have emerged through centuries of belief and practice. Still, our focus will be on spells specifically designed to assist in healing the sick and bring serenity to a troubled soul.

Whether you or a loved one are battling physical or mental health challenges, these spells may offer guidance and support on your journey toward healing. While these spells can serve as helpful tools in the healing process, it is vital to prioritize professional medical treatment. These spells should be viewed as an extra resource, not a substitute for proper medical care, to aid your wellness path. Remember always to seek qualified medical assistance when dealing with health concerns.

You can perform this spell to aid in the healing of someone who is physically ill or recovering from an injury. Begin by lighting a candle and placing a photo of the person who needs healing next to the candle. If you are the person in need of healing, place your own photo next to the candle. Say their name with the intention of promoting healing for either yourself or the other person.

Recite this incantation: "Candle of light guide me in healing both the mind and body of (name of person). Let your flame ignite the spark of healing and illuminate his/her path to recovery. I beseech my spirit guides and ancestors for their strength on this road to good health."

Repeat this spell every day until you see an improvement in the person's health. Remember to encourage them to care for themselves, nourish their body and soul, and follow their doctor's advice.

Do not fear if you are locked in battle with a pesky ailment, such as the relentless flu or the common cold. For there is helpful relief within reach – Vicks' Vapo Rub and magick. With just a touch of this enchanting ointment, your body may quicken the virus's departure from your system.

Stand before a mirror and generously apply Vicks' Vapo Rub to your chest, let out a deep breath, and speak these words with unwavering conviction:

"Chest cold, head cold, or flu, whatever you may be, hear me now and witness my unwavering will. Be gone from me, and let me be free."

Visualize the illness being forcefully pushed out of your body as you utter these words. And every morning and evening, repeat this ritual until you feel renewed and revitalized.

As the scent of eucalyptus and menthol fills the air, imagine yourself being cleansed of all sickness and restored to good health once again.

During times of worry and fear, our immune systems may weaken, leaving us susceptible to illness. To combat these feelings, it is beneficial to cultivate a sense of tranquility from within. Seek out a serene and secure environment where you can sit undisturbed, surrounded by the calming embrace of nature or the familiar comforts of your home.

Gently light a candle with a soothing scent, perhaps lavender or vanilla, or light some fragrant incense that brings you joy. Close your eyes and allow yourself to settle into this serene setting – a cozy room filled with memories of laughter and contentment.

Allow your mind to wander freely for a few moments, like a butterfly fluttering from flower to flower. Allow the warmth of the flickering flame and the comforting scents to envelop you in a peaceful embrace. When you feel relaxed, slowly recite these words,

"May my mind be cleansed of all worries and fears; may only thoughts of happiness enter, leaving my body and mind calm."

Open your eyes and focus on the flickering flame before you. Mentally set your intention for a calm and peaceful mind. Let the comforting scent of the candle and incense fill your senses and guide you toward a state of inner peace.

While taking care of our physical health is important, it is not the sole aspect of overall well-being that requires attention. For those struggling with mental health concerns, this incantation offers an opportunity to find peace and calm in the mind.

Find a peaceful, comfortable spot to sit and light a candle, then look into your reflection in a mirror. As you chant the spell, imagine a comforting embrace surrounding you and feel all your worries and fears melting away like wax from a candle. If you are performing this spell for someone else, place a photo of them on the mirror and recite these words:

"May this flame bring tranquility and calm to (person's name). Let it soothe their emotions, bringing clarity and peacefulness within. As the flame burns, any worries or fears may dissipate. May this light restore their inner peace and clear their mind."

As you say these words, visualize your or your loved one's mind becoming calmer and clearer, free from any struggles they may be facing. Repeat this spell daily until you notice an improvement in your or their emotional well-being. Remember also to be encouraged to seek professional help and support on the journey towards better mental health.

Harnessing the power of magick and making wise decisions can greatly benefit you in the long run. But don't forget that the simple act of getting out in nature has countless advantages for both the mind and body. Slowly walking through nature trails or strolling through peaceful parks not only relaxes your mind and calms your nerves but also provides numerous physical health benefits.

Walking lowers blood pressure, and a little exercise reduces the risk of heart disease. In addition to cardiovascular benefits, walking also strengthens your body's muscles and bones, helping prevent injuries. Simple walking can be a great form of exercise for weight loss and overall body wellness. But walking in nature benefits more than just your physical health.

As you engage in physical movement and soak up the beauty of the natural world around you, your brain releases endorphins – chemicals that induce feelings of pleasure and positivity. This consistent activity can also help alleviate symptoms of mental health issues like depression and anxiety, resulting in a more focused mind and uplifted spirit. Magick comes from nature that surrounds you. Take time to become one with the universe, and open your eyes to the wonders that are all around you.

In order to contribute effectively to your community, it is important to prioritize taking care of yourself. This means addressing your own needs before trying to solve problems for others, even close family members. It may seem selfish, but it is necessary for maintaining a healthy mind and body. Try to eat nutritious food (although this can be challenging), engage in moderate physical activity like walking a few times a week, and make time for self-reflection or meditation. Your future self will appreciate the effort.

Spells can also be used to maintain a healthy mind and body and shield against negative energy or illnesses. This particular spell harnesses the power of water, known for its cleansing and purifying abilities. Begin by filling a small bowl with water and lighting a candle beside it. As you recite these words,

"Element of water, pure and clean, protect and heal my body and soul. Let all negativity and illness wash away, leaving me healthy and whole,"

visualize the water washing away any impurities or negative energy from your being. Take a sip of the water as a symbol of taking in healing properties from the spiritual realm.

Repeat this spell weekly or whenever needed for an extra boost of protection and healing. Remember always to use spells with a pure heart and positive intentions.

Sometimes, neither modern medicine nor magick can heal a broken mind or body. During these moments, we must accept what we cannot change. Our lives have a unique path. We are on this earth to learn and to teach others from our experiences. Coping with a significant health issue or witnessing someone else's suffering is a part of this journey. Although difficult, we must try to understand the purpose behind the pain.

During the toughest moments, when acceptance feels like an insurmountable task, turn to this spell for solace. Find a tranquil and secure space, and speak these words as often as needed:

"The ebb and flow of life is constant. People enter and exit our lives. Through hardship, I will discover the strength to evolve. Acceptance is my sole choice; I gratefully welcome all that unfolds before me."

May these spells and your inner strength bring you and those dear to you abundant well-being and joy.

Blessed be.

CHAPTER 7: LOVE & RELATIONSHIPS

L ove and hate, two of the most potent and consuming emotions that guide our existence, have the power to sway our choices without us even realizing it. As powerful as Magick may be, it is impossible for any spell to compel someone to fall in love with another against their will. The heart is a sacred entity that cannot be tampered with by any form of craft or charm – it is a delicate balance of emotions, desires, and connections.

It is of utmost importance to always wield magick responsibly and with the intention of promoting goodness and harmony in the world. It cannot be used to control others, for that goes against the very essence of magick itself. This chapter contains a collection of spells crafted to help manifest love in your life. These enchantments are not meant to coerce or manipulate others but rather to foster self–love and strengthen the bonds between two consenting adults.

Before seeking love from another, it is crucial to cultivate love within oneself—recognizing one's worth and treating oneself with kindness and compassion. This solidifies a strong foundation for a loving and fulfilling relationship with another. These spells are not tools of control but rather tools of empowerment in the pursuit of love and happiness.

Through careful intention and a positive attitude, these spells can draw forth the universe's energy and align it with our desires for love, creating an atmosphere ripe for blossoming connections and heartfelt unions.

The following spell is one of self-nurturing and empowerment. Each morning, stand in front of a mirror with a conviction of empowerment. Gently caress your face, feeling the warmth of your skin and the strength in your hands. As you gaze deeply into your own eyes, repeat these empowering words:

"I infuse myself with boundless love and positivity, for I am worthy and deserving of all good things. My heart radiates with self-love, nourishing my mind, body, and soul."

Let these affirmations sink deep into your being like the roots of a tree growing stronger each day. Embrace yourself fully and reaffirm your worth and value. While receiving love from others is a beautiful thing, remember that your love for yourself is more powerful to achieve true happiness. It will bring profound peace and fortitude to every aspect of your life, blossoming like a garden in full bloom. It's a beautiful sight to behold.

Make a habit of repeating this spell whenever needed, especially during moments of low self-esteem or when facing challenges that test your confidence. Your love for yourself will always be a guiding light through any darkness.

If you find yourself feeling unfulfilled in your current relationship? This love spell may help reignite the spark between you and your partner, bringing back the passion and love that may have dimmed over time. Take a cherished photo of the two of you and place it before you in front of a lit candle. Close your eyes and imagine the soft glow of the candlelight illuminating the image, casting a warm and loving aura around the both of you.

As you repeat these words, let the emotion behind each syllable fuel your intention:

"Our love is strong, unbreakable even in the face of trials. As each day passes, I promise to place your happiness before mine and ask the same of you. Together, we are united in body, mind, and soul."

At night, as you drift into sleep, visualize a powerful and unbreakable bond between you and your partner. See threads of a white light connecting your hearts, strengthening your connection and bringing you closer together. Have faith that this spell will bring you closer to the deep and lasting love that you desire.

If you and your partner have grown distant or if there are unresolved issues within the relationship, it may be beneficial to seek guidance from a professional relationship counselor in addition to casting the above spell. Magick can help, but sometimes, outside support is necessary for healing and strengthening a bond.

For those seeking to find a new love, this spell may assist in attracting them into your life. However, it is essential to make sure you are mentally, emotionally, and financially stable before pursuing any potential relationships.

It's important to be content with being alone and have a solid foundation before jumping into dating or a new partnership.

When you feel you are ready to love and be loved, begin by composing a list of the attributes you desire in a partner. Take your time and delve deeply into your innermost desires, not just the shallow aspects of physical attraction or material possessions. Once you know what you truly want, light a candle and hold the list close to your heart, visualizing your future companion. Recite these words,

"I call upon my spirit guides. Bring me the love I seek—someone who will love and cherish me, with whom I can grow and share my life. May our souls become one."

Put the list in a sacred location, and have faith in your spirit guides to bring you the love necessary for your well-being—not just what you may want, but what you need.

One of the most powerful tools for attracting love is the practice of visualization and manifestation. Take a few moments each day to close your eyes and immerse yourself in a vivid picture of being in a truly fulfilling and loving relationship. See yourself surrounded by warmth, affection, and understanding from a partner who cherishes you. Allow your mind to embrace these positive thoughts and feelings. As you visualize this ideal relationship, let your heart swell with hope and anticipation for what lies ahead.

If your relationship is going through a difficult time and your partner is receptive to magick, this spell may aid in bringing peace and understanding between you. Begin by lighting a candle and sitting facing each other.

Visualize a warm, loving light surrounding both of you. As you join hands, recite these words together:

"Our hearts are open to love and understanding. May our love grow stronger through peace and compassion. Let our differences be resolved and bring us closer together. We are united in the power of love."

Allow the candle to burn out, trusting that the spell has fostered understanding and harmony in your relationship. Remember, while magick can be a powerful tool for inviting love and happiness into our lives, cultivating and maintaining healthy and loving relationships is ultimately up to us. It takes work and communication.

Long-term relationships, whether with friends or family, can be challenging at times. Even when you love each other deeply, there will be moments when you may get on each other's nerves; this is especially true for siblings. However, forgiving each other for any unintentional hurts in these relationships is crucial.

We all have bad days and can unintentionally hurt those we care about when we're feeling down. Try to be mindful of your words and tone when having a rough day. I find that taking a moment to meditate in a quiet place helps me manage my emotions instead of lashing out at others. Of course, we all make mistakes, so it's important to apologize and forgive whenever necessary.

This spell can bring peace and forgiveness to mend any strained or conflicted relationship. Begin by taking deep breaths to ground yourself. Close your eyes and channel your energy towards the person you wish to reconcile with. Then, recite these words:

"I invoke the elements of fire, water, air, earth, and spirit, surround us and release all tension. I let go of my anger, hurt, and resentment towards you. I offer my forgiveness and ask for the same from you. May our bond be strengthened through understanding and peace. So it shall be."

Visualize the tension between you and the person dissolving, being replaced with feelings of serenity and forgiveness. Trust that the spell will bring healing and reconciliation to your relationship.

Whether searching for a new love, strengthening a current bond, or yearning for forgiveness and healing, these spells will guide you on your journey. Always approach them with pure intentions, for love and happiness are precious gifts that should never be taken lightly.

Love and forgiveness have the ability to transform relationships and ignite profound change within ourselves and our connections with others. Nurturing these forces within ourselves can cultivate a world of compassion and understanding.

Genuine love thrives on mutual respect and trust. The pillars of strong relationships are built upon open communication and genuine understanding. By incorporating these essential values into our interactions, we can create harmonious and enriching bonds that stand the test of time.

May these spells bring you closer to the love and happiness you seek, and may all of your relationships be filled with joy, understanding, and mutual respect.

So let it be.

CHAPTER EIGHT

CHAPTER 8: CAREER

I n our society, there is often an excessive focus on
self-worth based solely on one's career or job title. However, it is vital to remind ourselves that our worth as individuals extends far beyond the limitations of our work.
While our profession may play a significant role in our lives
and how we are perceived by others, it does not define us
entirely.

We are multifaceted beings with many talents, passions,
and life experiences that shape who we are. It is crucial to
embrace the notion that our value lies not just in our occu-
pation but also in our inherent qualities, relationships, personal growth, and our positive impact on the world around
us. Our worth cannot be reduced to a single label or title; it
is a complex and dynamic culmination of all that makes us
unique individuals.

Work is just one small thread in the rich tapestry of our
lives, weaving its way alongside other important aspects
like family, hobbies, and self-care.

It is a piece of the puzzle, not the whole picture. Therefore, it is essential to strive for balance in all areas, cultivate our passions and pursuits outside of work, nurture and cherish our relationships with loved ones, and prioritize our physical, mental, and emotional well-being.

When we embrace our multidimensional selves and recognize that we are more than just a job title, our true essence shines brightly like a vibrant prism reflecting the many colors of who we are. Of course, while work should not define us, it still plays a significant role in our overall sense of fulfillment and happiness. And while magick cannot guarantee job success, it can help guide us towards opportunities and success in our chosen career path.

By incorporating magick into our daily lives, we can harness the power of unseen forces and connect with the right opportunities and pathways for personal and professional growth.

The journey toward career success starts with introspection and setting clear goals. Pause and delve deeply into your innermost desires, considering the type of work that truly ignites your passion. Envision yourself reaching new heights in your professional path. Ensure that your past experiences and education align with your desired career choice. Create a detailed list of your aspirations and keep them at the forefront of your thoughts as we embark on the following spells, channeling their energy towards manifesting your dreams into reality.

Our initial spell focuses on job searching and achieving our ideal career. Start by creating a sigil or vision board – a collection of written phrases, visuals, or icons that embody your dream job or professional journey.

A sigil holds great strength and can aid in bringing about your innermost wishes.

After you have finished creating your sigil, find a secure and sacred location to display it. Light a candle and sit facing the sigil, visualizing yourself excelling in your dream job with joy and fulfillment. As you recite the following words, hold onto that empowering emotion in your heart:

"Through the power of this sigil, I open myself to abundant opportunities in my desired career (state the specific job you seek). May my spirit guides lead me toward the perfect career path. So let it be."

Have faith in the strength of your intentions and the vision board you have constructed to draw job opportunities that match your abilities.

Is your current job eroding your happiness and making you feel stuck and suffocated, like a witch being punished in old Salem? It may be time to break free and seek new opportunities. This next spell is meant to guide you toward a job that not only satisfies your financial needs but also brings joy and fulfillment back into your work life.

Begin by finding a secluded spot outdoors, digging a small hole, and placing a candle inside. As you light the flame, repeat these words with conviction:

"With the powers of fire and earth, I release myself from the chains that bind me in my current job. I am open to new opportunities. Let this candle guide me towards a fulfilling career, and let my feet walk the ground towards a new chapter in my professional journey."

Visualize yourself breaking free from your current job and stepping confidently towards a bright future filled with satisfaction and purpose.

Let the warmth of the candle's flame ignite a newfound sense of hope and determination within you. Trust in the power of the elements to attract new opportunities and guide you to the perfect job.

Let us now embark on a journey of manifestation, using a spell to bring abundance and success into your current or future job. This potent magick can also be utilized to dismiss negativity and foster positive energy in a toxic work environment.

Begin by finding a small bowl, preferably crafted from earthy materials such as clay, and fill it with pure white salt, symbolizing the grounding powers of the earth. Light a candle next to the bowl, its flickering flame radiating warmth and passion. As you speak these words aloud,

"By the power of earth and fire, I call forth success and prosperity into my life. I banish all negative energies from my workplace and invite harmony to reign supreme. May my work thrive and flourish in this purified space. So it shall be."

Imagine the salt absorbing all the toxic energy in your workplace, leaving only positivity and fertile ground for growth and success. Leave the candle and salt bowl in your office or workspace for maximum potency. The smell of burning wax and cleansing salt will remind you of your intentions and attract abundant blessings into your professional life.

Now, let's explore a spell for career advancement and growth. This spell can be performed to manifest a promotion, salary increase, or any other form of career progress. Write your specific career goal on a piece of paper and fold it three times before placing it in your wallet.

Take a candle and carve your desired outcome onto its wick, such as "promotion" or "raise." Light the candle and recite these words:

"I call upon my ancestors and spirit guides to bless me with success and growth in my career. May my talents be acknowledged and rewarded, and may I achieve my ultimate goal. So let it be."

As the flame flickers, visualize yourself attaining your goal and feel the excitement and satisfaction that comes with it. Keep the folded paper in your wallet as a reminder of your intentions and a source of magical support.

As you cast these spells, remember that they will aid and guide you toward achieving your career goals. However, the true power lies in your determination, hard work, and dedication to seek the necessary training for success in your desired field. Let your intentions infuse each spell, trusting in the vastness of the universe to bring about the fulfillment and triumph you crave while applying a strong work ethic.

As the last phase of your career approaches, the thought of retirement may seem like a dream. However, retirement doesn't have to be just a fantasy or nightmare. Retirement is not only about stepping away from daily work for income but also about finding joy and balance in your new chapter of life.

If you're feeling ready to move on from your current career and retire or yearn for more fulfillment in your work life, this spell will guide you toward manifesting that transition. Before you begin your work day, recite these words:

"I call upon the wisdom of my ancestors and the gods of prosperity to bless me with abundance and financial independence. May my investments thrive and savings flourish, ensuring a future where I am truly thriving."

As you recite these words, visualize yourself living a happy and abundant retirement – surrounded by loved ones, pursuing your passions and interests without any financial worries. Trust in the strength of this spell to draw you closer to this desired reality."

Your career journey should bring success, achievement, balance, and fulfillment to your life. Preparing for retirement is crucial as you progress toward your goals and work hard to build a secure future.

The true measure of success and contentment in career and retirement lies in taking care of yourself holistically, living within your means, and prioritizing your mental and physical well-being. May these spells guide your path towards a prosperous and satisfying life filled with abundance and joy.

Work hard, but play harder. On your path to success, remember to take time out for the people in your life. True success comes from love, not money.

CHAPTER NINE

CHAPTER 9: SPIRIT GUIDES

The presence of spirits lingers around us, unseen but felt. Some possess an innate ability to connect with these beings; some call them ghosts, allowing these special people to see and communicate with the spirit realm effortlessly. For others, it may require honing their skills through magick and opening themselves up to the supernatural world to establish communication. Whether it be a natural gift or a learned skill, the connection to the spirit world is one of mystery and wonder.

Our ancestors hold immense power as spirits, capable of guiding and protecting us even in death. Having lived through the same bloodline and endured similar struggles, they possess wisdom and insight that can greatly benefit our lives. Connecting with our ancestors allows us to delve deeper into our family history, gain a valuable understanding of our current lives, and pay tribute to those who paved the way for our current opportunities.

When death claims a person, their soul is faced with a decision: to journey into the unknown realms of the afterlife or linger as a spectral presence in the land of the living. For most, the love and loyalty they hold for those left behind compels them to become guardians, watching over their loved ones from beyond.

But in rare and troubling circumstances, other forces may intervene and impede their journey, leaving them trapped in a cycle of existence as restless ghosts, unable to find peace in the afterlife or move on from the moment of their untimely demise. The confusion and turmoil of this state may prove to be a haunting burden, both for the spirits themselves and those who encounter them.

The first spell in this chapter will assist you in establishing a connection and opening communication with your ancestors. Begin by lighting a candle over a photograph or object that belonged to one of your ancestors. Concentrate your intention on connecting with your ancestors. Recite these words:

"I invoke my ancestors, (Name(s) of the person(s)); may your spirit guide me. Help me see and comprehend the world around me. May our bond strengthen as we walk this path together. So let it be."

Sit in quietly for a few minutes, focusing on the person(s) in the photo and allowing their messages to come through. When you feel connected, express gratitude and extinguish the candle.

For those unsure of their heritage or who have been adopted, this spell can help you connect with your biological ancestors.

Begin by taking a candle and carving the word "ancestors" into it. Light the candle and place it next to a mirror. As you gaze into the mirror, recite these words:

"By the light of this flame, I call upon my bloodline to reveal the path of my true ancestry. May their spirits guide me and bring clarity and understanding into my life."

Imagine a warm and nurturing light surrounding you as you look into the mirror, inviting your biological ancestors to appear before you. Allow yourself to open up and receive any thoughts, feelings, or visions that may come through as you meditate on your ancestral ties. When you feel ready to close the spell, express gratitude to those who came before you and blow out the candle.

In many spiritual practices, it is important to honor deceased family members. This spell helps you create a special space in your home dedicated to your ancestors, where you can pay tribute to their memory and seek guidance from their spirits.

Find a quiet spot in your house and gather objects representing your ancestors, such as photos, heirlooms, or keepsakes. Arrange these items on a table or shelf, creating a sacred area for your ancestral altar. Light a candle and recite these words:

"I give reverence to those who came before me. May their love and guidance illuminate my path. As I pay homage, may their spirits watch over and protect me. So let it be."

Take a moment to reflect upon the items on your altar, feeling the weight of history and the presence of those who have passed on. Each photograph and heirloom holds a story, a memory, a piece of the puzzle that is your heritage.

Our spirit guides may not always be related to us by blood; they could also be spirits who cross our path and feel a strong connection with us. These guides can take many forms, some appearing as animals and becoming familiar companions (which will be discussed in another chapter), others showing themselves as angels, or even taking on the form of a child's imaginary friend.

Spirit guides serve as mentors and guardians on our spiritual journey, offering guidance, protection, and support. Some may stay with us for our entire lives, while others may come and go depending on our individual needs and circumstances. It is important to distinguish between calling upon our spirit guides during magickal workings and communicating with ghosts of the dead, which we will delve into later on.

To connect with your spirit guides, it is important to approach the process with respect and an open mind. The following spell is crafted to summon their presence and invite their wisdom into your life. Find a comfortable space where you can relax undisturbed. Light a candle and take a few deep breaths to center yourself. Then, speak these words aloud:

"Spirits that guide me I honor and thank you. Lead me towards happiness and protect me from harm. In your infinite knowledge, show me the way to inner peace."

As you say these words, envision a soothing light surrounding you, drawing in the guidance and energy of your spirit guides. Embrace their influence as you remain receptive to their presence.

After establishing a sense of connection with spirit, meditate and listen for any guidance or insights that may emerge. Have faith in your spirit guides' wisdom and be receptive to their assistance in whatever way it presents itself.

Remember that your spirit guides are here to help and uplift you on your journey. Approach them with appreciation and reverence. With their guidance, clarity, and assurance, you can navigate life's obstacles.

Pursuing magick can enhance our lives in various aspects, such as love, career, and connecting with spirits. This journey is deeply individual and can bring personal growth and enrichment. Each spell shared here aims to empower, heal, and promote development.

Self-love is essential for building healthy relationships in the realm of love. By recognizing our own worth and nurturing self-compassion, we attract more fulfilling connections with others. Self-love reminds us that true love starts from within. If you struggle with this area, seeking guidance from your spirit guides may help improve your self-worth.

If you desire a boost in self-confidence, this spell may call upon your spirit guides to provide assistance. Stand before a mirror and take a few deep breaths to ground yourself. Then, recite these words:

"Spirit guides who walk beside me; I ask for your wisdom and illumination. Please guide me as I strive for self-love. Help me recognize my value and inner strength. I am worthy of love. May your presence uplift and motivate me each day."

Observe yourself as you allow the spell's energy to settle within you. Feel the support and encouragement of your spirit guides as you embark on your journey towards self-love and assurance.

As you reflect on the wise teachings of your ancestors and spirit guides, it is essential to hold them in the highest regard and show them gratitude. The bond you create with spirit is sacred and deserves the utmost respect.

When seeking guidance or assistance from those who have departed the land of the living, it is crucial to approach them with humility and appreciation. They offer us their wisdom and unwavering support, and honoring their presence allows for a deep and profound connection. May we continue to be blessed by the divine influence of our ancestors and spirit guides.

In order to honor and connect with your spirit guides, make it a daily practice to acknowledge them with genuine gratitude and love. They are always by your side, listening and offering guidance; do not only turn to them in moments of desperation but also take time to show appreciation for their presence and wisdom. As you express your gratitude, bask in the deep connection that exists between you and your guides.

Close your eyes, and allow yourself to feel the gentle and loving energy of your spirit guides enveloping you like a warm embrace. Their presence is like a comforting blanket, always surrounding you and offering their infinite wisdom and guidance on your journey. With each word of gratitude that flows from your heart, let it be infused with boundless love for these divine beings who have chosen to walk beside you every step of the way.

Embrace this moment of connection and bask in the warmth of their radiant love.

CHAPTER TEN

CHAPTER 10: KARMA

K arma, the spiritual law of cause and effect, governs the energy that we release into the universe. Every action thought, and intention has a ripple effect that eventually returns to us in some form or another. In this chapter, we will delve into the practice of casting magick spells to influence the karma for both ourselves and others. By tapping into this force, we can manifest positive changes in our lives and the lives of those around us.

Karma is not just a vague concept; it is the pulsating life force of existence. It threads through our thoughts, words, and deeds, intricately woven into the fabric of our being and constantly reflecting back to us. Like a shimmering mirror, it magnifies the energy we emit, reverberating with our intentions in its own unique rhythm. Understanding karma is not about fearing repercussions but rather embracing the opportunity for growth and rebirth. It is a constant flow of cause and effect, offering the chance for personal transformation and rejuvenation.

In the realm of magick, the concept of karma holds great weight. It is the understanding that all things are connected, and with every action we take, there is a ripple effect that can impact ourselves and others. Within the magical community, there is much debate surrounding the rule of three – a belief that karma will return to us threefold. In other words, for every harm we cause, we will experience three times more suffering than the person we harmed.

In this chapter, we will not delve into the exact consequences that may arise from our actions and spells, but it is important to recognize that they will impact us in some way. The spells presented here are intended to guide us towards positive intentions and outcomes, promoting balance and harmony within ourselves and in the world around us. We must approach them with caution and responsibility, aware of the power they hold and their potential effects on our karmic journey.

Let's first explore a spell designed to send positive energy to someone who may be in need. Take a moment to ground yourself and focus on the individual you want to send this positive karma to. Light a candle and recite these words:

"I call on the elements earth, wind, fire, water, and spirit, and by your power, send forth positive karma to [name(s) of the person(s). May they be surrounded by love, light, and abundance, And may their path be filled with happiness and peace. As I sow shall they receive, so it shall be."

It's important to remember that karma operates in subtle and often mysterious ways, and the effects of this spell may not always be immediately apparent. You should see the spell's effects and your love take root in time.

Mirror magic can be a powerful tool in reflecting energies, including karma. Here is a simple mirror spell to help someone receive the karma they deserve. Begin by finding a small mirror that you can comfortably hold. Find a quiet place where you won't be disturbed. Hold the mirror and focus on the person you want to reflect karma onto. Envision their actions and intentions being mirrored back to them, whether positive or negative, as you recite these words:

"Mirror, reflecting thy heart, send back the energy they do. Let happiness be bestowed for good deeds, and let harm be returned for malicious intentions. May they reap what they have sown."

Imagine the mirror reflecting back everything that person has done. Trust in the power of this spell to bring about appropriate karma for them. Once you feel that the spell is complete, express gratitude to the universe.

Mirrors hold great power, for they are portals to our inner selves. If you find yourself struggling with a difficult person and the previous spell has not yielded results, it may be time to take things up a notch. For this spell, you will need a compact mirror, which can easily be found at any store that sells makeup. Make sure to get one with two mirrors inside.

On one side of the mirror, write the name(s) of the person(s) you wish to reflect karma onto in REVERSAL/MIRROR writing (writing from right to left). If you cannot find a double-sided mirror, simply tape a piece of paper with the name on the opening side. On the other side, write the word RETURN in upright writing (writing from left to right). Close the mirror and light three candles to symbolize your intentions. Then, speak these words:

"By the power of karma, I ask the universe to reflect the deeds and words from [name(s) of person(s)] back to them. May they see the wrong they have done and learn from their actions. Harm none, so let it be."

Look into the mirror and visualize all the karma they put out into the world returning back to them. Take satisfaction in knowing they will eventually reap what they sow.

When you feel the spell is complete, blow out the candles. Keep the mirror in a safe place, as you may need to use it again in the future. Be mindful of your intentions and approach this spell with respect and a desire for a positive resolution, not to bring harm but to help them be the best they can be.

Karma also applies to ourselves, and it's essential to recognize when we have done wrong and take steps towards forgiveness and restoration. The following spell involves self-reflection and seeking forgiveness from the universe for any harm we have caused. Start by considering how your words or actions may have caused harm to another person and why you put negative energy into the universe.

Then, find a quiet, comfortable space where you won't be disturbed. Light a candle and sit in front of it, allowing its flame to draw your focus. Take several deep breaths to center yourself and bring your attention inward. As you reflect on your actions, recite these words,

"I call on my higher power with humility and remorse. I acknowledge the harm I have caused through my words and actions towards myself and others. I ask for forgiveness and guidance as I strive to do better. May my intentions be pure as I walk through life-giving love and kindness in all I do."

Visualize your spirit guides surrounding you with a warm and forgiving light, offering guidance for your journey ahead. Feel the weight of your actions lifted as you release guilt or negativity.

Once you feel a sense of peace and acceptance, express gratitude to the universe for its forgiveness. Blow out the candle, symbolizing the end of this ritual and the beginning of a new chapter of growth and healing.

Remember, karma is not a punishment for our actions but an opportunity for growth and learning. By acknowledging our mistakes and actively seeking redemption, we can align ourselves with positive energies and create a brighter future for ourselves and those around us.

Let us move forward on our journey towards a better life, understanding that the principles of karma will always play a role in our spiritual practice. The spells shared throughout this chapter are tools to aid you on your path toward healing, empowerment, and growth. However, it's important to remember that they are not the only way to achieve these goals; each individual's spiritual journey is unique, and it's essential to find what resonates best with you.

Trust in the power of your intentions and your connection to the spiritual realm, and allow these spells to guide and assist you in manifesting your desires. May your path be illuminated by love, peace, and abundance as you continue on your journey through life.

If you ever find yourself consumed by negativity and behaving like a "Karen," this spell may be just what you need. Stand before a mirror, gazing into your own reflection, and recite these words:

"I call upon my ancestors and spirit guides to heal the pain within my heart. May I never cause harm to others through my words or actions. Protect me from the consequences of any harm I may inflict upon others. Let only positivity flow from me in both word and deed. Blessed Be"

Envision yourself letting go of any negative feelings or behavior. Embrace your true positive and loving self, and know that with the help of your spirit guides and ancestors, you can overcome negativity and spread love into the world.

You must always be mindful of the energy we put out into the world and strive for positivity and balance in all aspects of our lives. By harnessing the power of karma and our connection to the spiritual realm, we can manifest positive change in ourselves and in the world around us.

CHAPTER 11: FAMILIAR

A ccording to the Oxford Dictionary, a familiar is a demon that serves and follows a witch, often taking on the appearance of an animal. While this definition is partially correct, familiars can also be associated with practitioners of magic in general, not just witches. They are animals or spirits linked to individuals who practice magic, playing a vital role in different facets of their human life.

Familiars are considered to be spirits who take on animal form when they return from the realm of the dead, choosing to serve as companions rather than remaining as spirit guides.

Throughout history, the depiction of familiars has been ever-changing, their role in magick shifting and evolving. Some traditions have painted them as malevolent beings, evil spirits or demons bound to the will of a witch or sorcerer. Other belief systems see familiars in a more positive light, as benevolent spirit guides that offer protection and aid to the practitioner in their magical endeavors.

Whether one believes in their existence or not, familiars hold a significant place in mystical spiritualism. These unique companions have a captivating effect on those who seek their wisdom and understanding. Their impact cannot be denied, leaving a lasting mark on all who connect with them during spiritual practices involving magick.

In this chapter, we will delve into the bonds between practitioners and their familiar. Whether you are a firm believer in spirits or not, the connection between human and animal companions is undeniably powerful. Together, they work towards the betterment of one's life.

The first crucial step in working with a familiar is finding one that closely aligns with your being. Take into account your personal preferences and any animals that hold significant meaning in your life. For instance, if you have always been drawn to the grace and independence of cats, a sleek feline familiar may be the ideal companion for you. Their piercing eyes and silent movements evoke a sense of mystique and power that may resonate deeply with your soul.

To invite a familiar into your life, you can perform a spell or set an intention to attract one. Another way to attract them is to create a space in your home dedicated to them. This can be a designated area or an altar adorned with items representing the animal you wish to connect with. Offerings and symbols, such as food, toys, and images, can be placed in this space to entice and honor the animal spirit.

You can also leave out offerings of your own, such as a lock of hair, a piece of clothing, or a trinket. Once you have set up the space, take the time to sit and meditate in front of it. Visualize the animal spirit you wish to connect with and invite them into your life.

Express your intentions for wanting a familiar and your willingness to bond and work with them.

Be patient and open-minded, as the animal spirit may take some time to make its presence known. If you feel a particular pull towards a specific animal, whether through dreams, signs, or gut feelings, it could be a sign that it is familiar to you. Acknowledge this intuitive feeling and nurture your connection with the animal spirit.

Another way to connect with a familiar is through a spell work. Gather items representing the animal you wish to communicate with, such as feathers, fur, or images of the animal. Find a quiet and private space to perform the spell without interruption.

After you have gathered your items, light a candle and place them around it. Sit in front of the flickering flame, close your eyes, and take deep breaths to ground yourself. Visualize a protective light surrounding you, and within this light, envision the animal spirit you wish to connect with. As you speak these words from your heart, feel the presence of your spirit guides:

"Respected and loved spirit guides, I call upon you to send me an animal familiar that I may bond within this living realm. May they walk beside me and offer guidance and companionship on my journey through this life."

Close your eyes and take several deep breaths to center yourself. Visualize a protective circle of light surrounding you. Then, visualize your ideal familiar approaching you. Invite them to join you in your circle and communicate with them telepathically. Ask them questions and listen for their responses. Trust in your intuition and the messages you receive.

Another method for finding a familiar is to spend time in nature, connecting with the natural world and the spirits that reside there. Pay attention to any animals or signs that catch your eye, as they may be messages from your familiar. Practice mindfulness and open yourself to receiving guidance from the spirits around you.

Another spell to help attract your spirit guide in animal form, go out to the forest, find a quiet spot, and visualize the type of animal that you feel is best suited for your lifestyle, and then recite these words:

"Ancestors, blood of my blood and Spirit guides who walk with me, I call upon you. Lead me through the darkness and into the light and bring me a familiar into my life."

Close your eyes and envision your trusted animal companion coming towards you. Their steps will be light and graceful as they move through the spirit realm. Feel a warm sense of connection and understanding between the two of you as you communicate your intentions to them.

Be patient and keep your senses open to receiving their messages and insights. Working alongside familiars is a sacred and powerful practice that should be approached with respect and gratitude for the significant role these animal spirits play in our lives.

To be selected by an animal to be your familiar is a great honor, one that signifies a deep connection and potential for powerful magick. But this is only the beginning. Establish a bond between you and your familiar, who is not just any animal but a cherished companion and valued family member. They are more than just ordinary pets; they should hold a special place in your heart and soul, guiding and assisting you on your journey through life.

Familiars play a vital role in our lives, acting as trusted allies and guides through the realm of magick. With their unwavering trust and understanding, they aid us in channeling energies and directing them toward our intentions, exponentially strengthening the effectiveness of our spells. While they bring immense power to our practices, they also provide unconditional love and comfort in times of need.

Despite their portrayal in legends and old wives' tales, those with the privilege of a familiar's presence know the deep and unbreakable bond between practitioner and animal. It is a connection forged from unwavering trust and mutual respect, a bond that transcends words and surpasses any human–animal relationship. The familiar's presence is like a warm embrace, a tangible manifestation of the mystical world intertwined with our own. It is a bond that cannot be fully explained, only felt and cherished by those fortunate enough to experience it.

Familiars, whether they be cats, dogs, or other creatures, offer much more than just physical support. They provide a deep emotional and spiritual connection that can be felt in every aspect of life. When the world becomes chaotic and overwhelming, they are there to ground and center their human companion, offering comfort and stability like no other.

Their presence is like a warm blanket on a cold day, soothing and calming the mind and soul. It's no wonder that those who have experienced this bond see their familiar not just as an ally in magick but as a beloved friend in life.

However, it is important to remember that bringing any animal into your life is not a decision to be taken lightly.

It requires a long-term commitment of 15–20 years and significant financial resources to care for them properly.

As an animal caregiver, you are responsible for meeting all their needs – from providing food and shelter to showering them with love and attention. Before embarking on this journey, be sure to consider the dedication and responsibility it entails carefully.

In addition, it's important to remember that a familiar is not a toy or a tool for personal gain. They are living beings with their own needs and desires, and it is essential to treat them with love and respect. A familiar should never be forced into performing any action against their will, and their well-being should always be the top priority.

In conclusion, the bond between practitioner and familiar is sacred and powerful, rooted in mutual respect and understanding. Together, you walk the path of magick, enhancing each other's abilities and providing support and solace in moments of need. Whether you believe in their existence or not, familiars hold a place of great importance in mystical practices and should be honored and cherished accordingly.

CHAPTER 12: ACCEPTANCE

Throughout the ages, various societies and cultures have long vilified practitioners of magick for various reasons. In many religious contexts, particularly in Christianity, Islam, and Judaism, the practice of magic has been condemned as heretical or blasphemous. This opposition stems from the belief that magick involves communing with supernatural forces or entities outside the control of the one true deity, which challenges their religious authority and doctrine.

Magick often involves practices and beliefs that are not easily explained or understood by mainstream society. Fear of the unknown can lead to suspicion, prejudice, and persecution of those who practice magick. In times of instability, people may seek scapegoats and practitioners of magick have often been targeted as convenient targets.

Practitioners of magick have often been marginalized and stigmatized within society, labeled as witches, sorcerers, or warlocks.

These labels come with negative connotations and can lead to discrimination and even violence against those perceived to be practicing magick.

As you can see, being a practitioner of magick has its downside. If you wish to include magick in your spiritual life, you should be aware that the people around you may not understand and could be hostile towards you.

Learning to accept yourself and the choices you make to better your life is crucial, and magick can assist you in accepting that other people may never understand your spiritual journey. Here is a spell you can use to block the noise around you.

Light a candle in a quiet place where you won't be disturbed. Sit comfortably and take a few deep breaths to center yourself. In your mind, visualize a protective bubble surrounding you, shielding you from negative energies and people who do not support your spiritual practices. Recite these words,

"I call on the elements—air, water, fire, earth, and spirit—to shield me from negativity and judgment. I release the need for others' approval and embrace the spiritual path. My life, my truth. So let it be."

Visualize a warm light blocking out all negativity and judgment from others. When you feel ready, blow out the candle, symbolizing the end of the spell and the beginning of your journey toward self-acceptance. Trust in your own power and your connection to the spiritual realm. You do not need anyone else's approval or understanding to validate your beliefs and practices.

The spell you've performed to shield yourself from negativity and judgment is a powerful tool for maintaining your spiritual independence and inner peace. Remember to trust your intuition and connection to the spiritual realm, regardless of external influences or opinions.

As you continue your magickal journey, surround yourself with supportive, like-minded individuals who understand and respect your beliefs. Building a community of fellow practitioners can provide invaluable support and encouragement along the way.

Ultimately, the journey of a magick practitioner is one of self-discovery, empowerment, and spiritual growth. By embracing their unique gifts and perspectives, courage, resilience, and a steadfast belief in the power of magick, practitioners can overcome adversity, emerge stronger, and become authentic versions of themselves.

If you feel that you are having a hard time accepting yourself as you are, magick can assist, but you may want to consider talking with a licensed therapist as well. Acceptance and self-love are essential aspects of a healthy and fulfilling life.

With the support and guidance of magick and mental health professionals, you can overcome any challenge and embrace your true self. You are powerful and can conquer anything with the right tools and mindset.

Using spellwork for self-acceptance may not be an overnight process, but with consistent effort and trust in yourself, you will reach a place of self-love and confidence. The journey is just as important as the destination, and your spiritual growth and self-acceptance will continue to evolve and strengthen over time.

As you go about your daily life, remember to trust in your power and the power of magick to guide you towards self-acceptance. Embrace yourself as a unique and powerful being, and let the magick within you shine brightly. Believe in yourself always, for you are worthy and capable of greatness.

This spell is an invocation for self-empowerment and protection. It acknowledges the challenges faced by magick practitioners and offers a powerful tool for navigating those challenges while fostering self-acceptance and inner peace.

Visualize a protective bubble, a strong barrier against negativity and judgment from others. Open yourself up to encouragement and trust in your own power and connection to the spiritual realm, which reinforces a sense of inner strength and resilience. When you are ready, write down these words and recite them whenever you feel the need,

"I am a practitioner of magick, and I embrace my path with courage and conviction. With the elements as my shield, I am empowered to protect myself from all negative energies and judgment. I trust in my own power. So it shall be."

Carry this spell with you as a reminder that you are in control of your own journey and have the power to overcome any obstacles. You are worthy, unique, and have a place in the magick realm. Allow yourself to shine brightly and embrace your role as a powerful and capable magick practitioner.

Acceptance of oneself is an important part of living a healthy and happy life.

However, it is also important to be able to accept others for who they are. It is important to remember that we do not have the power to change other people, no matter how hard we try. Accepting others for who they are is essential for fostering understanding, compassion, and harmony in our relationships and communities.

In our wish to guide and support others on their journey, it's essential to recognize that true change comes from within. We can offer our love, encouragement, and resources, but ultimately, each individual is responsible for their own path and decisions.

Acceptance also plays a significant role in magick. Practitioners understand the importance of respecting others' beliefs and practices, even if they differ from their own. Magick is a deeply personal and diverse practice, and there is no one-size-fits-all approach. Embracing this diversity enriches the magickal community and fosters a sense of unity and mutual respect.

If you find it hard at times to accept someone's opinions or ideas that differ from your own, this spell may guide you to be more open. Sit or stand in front of a mirror to reflect your energy back to you and recite these words:

"I call upon my Spirit Guides for guidance, opening my mind and heart to new perspectives and understanding. Empower me with empathy and acceptance of diverse thoughts. Let it be so."

Continue to diligently repeat this spell whenever you feel yourself becoming closed off to the feelings and beliefs of others. Trust in the boundless power of magick to help you overcome any obstacles in your path and grow into a more compassionate and accepting individual.

As we embrace diversity and respect the unique beliefs and practices of each person, we can create a harmonious and united community that benefits all who are a part of it. Let these words guide you towards open-mindedness and understanding as you work towards building a kinder world for all beings.

It is not uncommon to feel small and insignificant in a world where everyone seems to be succeeding and achieving more than you. Constantly comparing your life to others can be a dangerous game, one that often leads to feelings of inadequacy and self-doubt.

Remember, your journey is unique and incomparable to anyone else's. Embrace your individuality and strive for personal growth instead of comparing yourself to others' accomplishments. Do not let the illusion of competition cloud your perception; instead, focus on your own path and all that you are capable of achieving along the way.

Stand tall in front of a mirror, your shoulders squared and your feet planted firmly on the ground. Take s few deep breaths in and exhale slowly out, then recite these words:

"I call on the elements Earth, Fire, Air, Water, and Spirit, steady my mind and not judge myself by what others have. I am walking my path and will allow you to lead me where I need to be."

Let go of any judgments about yourself based on comparisons to others. You are on your own unique path, guided by your own spirit guides. Trust that they will lead you exactly where you need to be in life.

CHAPTER 13: CALLING ON THE DEAD

I nteracting with the deceased is a unique experience, distinct from communicating with your spirit guides. This chapter aims to help you summon those who may be lingering within our realm, unable to move on or find purpose as guides for the living. Connecting with the dead can also grant insight into the spirit world.

One crucial element of conversing with the departed is approaching them with deep respect and reverence. These souls have departed from the physical realm, and their presence should be treated with utmost reverence and honor.

Before reaching out to the spirits of the deceased, it is crucial to prepare a sacred sanctuary where you can feel secure and sheltered. This could be a tranquil area in your home or a secluded corner outdoors.

Light fragrant candles that are pleasing to the senses or burning incense to conjure a serene ambiance and show reverence and respect to the spirits you wish to summon and engage with. The communication process. You may choose to use tools such as a pendulum, an Ouija board, a mirror, or simply meditation and visualization to connect with the spirits.

To call upon the spirits of the dead through a seance, gather a group of trusted friends who are open and respectful of the spirit world. Together, sit in a circle with a single candle placed in the center as your beacon to the other side. Invite the spirits you wish to communicate with into the circle, whether they be loved ones or benevolent entities from beyond.

If unsure, ask for friendly and kind spirits to join your gathering. In united voices and hearts full of respect for the dead, speak these words:

"Spirits of the departed, we beckon you to join us in this sacred circle. We seek only those who mean us no harm and carry messages of love and guidance. Please make your presence known to us."

As the words float through the air and dissipate into the unknown, be still and listen for any signs or responses from the other side. Feel their energies intertwine with yours as you open your mind and heart to their presence. And remember, always approach such rituals with caution and respect for those who have passed on.

After inviting the spirits, wait patiently and observe any signs of their presence. Some may feel an energy shift or hear whispers or sounds.

Others may have visions or feelings of the spirits' presence. You may then ask the spirit to swing the pendulum if you are using one, side to side if the answer is no, or circular if the answer is yes.

If you wish to communicate with a specific spirit, you can call out their name or a message you wish to convey. Trust that they will hear you and respond in their own way. Remember to approach the spirits respectfully and kindly, just as you would with living beings.

Each group member can take turns asking questions or sharing messages with the spirits. When you feel the communication has come to an end, thank the spirits for their presence and blow out the candle, symbolizing the end of the seance.

Take some time to reflect and discuss the experience as a group. Remember to close the circle by having each person say goodbye to the spirit. Showing respect and gratitude to the spirits during and after a seance is essential. They have taken the time to communicate with you and share their messages, and it's important to honor their presence and the knowledge they have imparted.

Preparing for a seance requires more than just gathering around a table and calling out to the spirits. It is a sacred ritual that demands a clear intention, an open mind, and a deep understanding of the responsibility of communicating with the dead. The veil between the living and the dead is delicate; proceed with caution and reverence.

The modern Ouija board is a commercial product created in the late 19th century. It was patented in 1890 by Kennard.

The name "Ouija" is said to have come from a combination of the French word "oui" (meaning "yes") and the German word "ja" (also meaning "yes").

In 1966, Parker Brothers acquired the rights to the Ouija board. They marketed it as a game rather than a tool for spiritual communication. Despite this, many people continued to use it for divination or attempting to contact spirits.

Before the Ouija board, as we know it, various forms of "talking boards" were used in spiritualist practices. These were often homemade and purportedly used by mediums during seances to receive messages from the spirit world.

If you choose to use an Ouija board with the planchet that comes with the game or a pendulum, there are a few general rules that many magick practitioners agree on. The first is the same as when attempting to speak to spirits: Approach the seance with respect and honor for the dead.

Eliminate distractions and ensure a quiet atmosphere. Clear your mind of negative thoughts and set a positive intention for the spell. Some people choose to say a prayer or perform a protective ritual before starting. Begin by opening the seance, which can involve everyone placing their fingers lightly on the planchette or board and asking for any spirits present to communicate.

Always remember to formally close the seance when you're finished to prevent any lingering connections, which could cause a spirit to attach to one of the participants. This is not the same as having a spirit choose you as someone to guide. When calling on the dead, you may bring forward a spirit guide; however, in most cases, you will speak with a spirit who does not know how to cross over and may feel trapped in one location.

It is also important to ask clear, specific questions during the seance. Avoid asking about negative or disturbing topics, as this can attract negative energy. It is best to ask yes or no questions, as answering them requires less energy from the spirit. Be patient and calm during the session. It may take time for the planchette to move, and the messages may come slowly.

You may also ask the spirit to knock on the table or wall. Ask for one knock for yes and two knocks for no. Responses may be faint, so you may need to ask the spirit to knock louder. Participants of the seance may bring personal items attached to a spirit they would like to contact.

Once a connection to the spirit world has been established, you may ask, "Good spirit, do you know anyone in this circle?" If you get a yes response, you may dive deeper into your questioning to determine the relationship to one of the participants.

Always remember that communication with the dead should not be taken lightly. If you feel uncomfortable or fearful during a seance, it is best to end the session immediately and close the circle. It is also wise to be with others when calling on the dead, as they can offer support and protection.

Whether you use an Ouija board or another form of divination to speak with the dead, always approach it with respect, caution, and clear intention. With an open mind, a positive attitude, and respectful energy, you can potentially connect with the spirits and receive messages from the other side. Stay safe, and always show gratitude for the spirits' presence and the messages they may share with you.

Attempting to call on spirits alone, especially in an area where someone has died tragically, is not recommended. If you find yourself in a situation where a spirit is reaching out to you, protect yourself from harm with this simple spell.

First, shield yourself mentally with a warm, comforting, powerful white light surrounding you. It will bend smoothly around you and protect you from harm.

Imagine a mirror that reflects the image of a spirit, prompting them to recognize their state and move forward. Some spirits are unaware of their passing and require assistance to transition to the next realm. They might not perceive their reflection accurately, unaware that it signifies their need to move on.

Recite these words: "Spirit, I guide you; embrace the light and allow it to take you to the other side, where you will find peace and purpose. So it shall be."

This spell should help the spirit to cross over and do no harm to you or others. Remember never to engage with negative or hostile spirits. Your safety and well-being should always come first when dealing with the spirit world.

If you are new to magick, it is best not to call on spirits through seances without someone with experience to guide you. This is for your safety and the safety of those who join in on the seance. As you become more experienced and comfortable with magick, you can expand your practice and knowledge to include working with spirits and communicating with the other side.

CHAPTER 14: HEX & CURSE

C urses and hexes are often used interchangeably, but they hold different meanings in the world of magic and folklore. Even though both are used for good and evil, their intentions, methods, and outcomes differ vastly.

Curses, steeped in the potency of emotion and intention, are often deliberate and directed, serving as a focused channel for invoking harm or misfortune upon a specific object. Conversely, hexes are more generalized and pervasive, casting a broader net of affliction upon a person. Despite these nuances, curses and hexes share a common thread of invoking forces to influence or harm a person.

One method of understanding this concept is to cast a curse on an object, such as a mirror, to reveal a person's true nature. This act imbues the mirror with the ability to reflect back a person's inner beauty or ugliness when they gaze upon their own reflection, a cursed object.

To hex someone is to cast a spell upon them, causing their true selves to be revealed through any reflective surface, putting a hex on a person.

The temptation to seek revenge or justice through hexes and curses may be alluring, but weighing the potential consequences of such actions is crucial. In almost every belief system and spiritual practice, one universal law remains constant: the energy you put into the world will return to you. Negative intentions and actions can create a domino effect, causing more harm and suffering for yourself and those around you.

Suppose your true desire is to bring about positive change in a situation. In that case, channeling your energy and focusing on promoting healing and growth rather than inflicting harm upon others is wiser. The universe constantly shifts and responds to our energies, so let us use that power wisely and consciously for the greater good.

In addition, it explores and utilizes alternative forms of magick, such as protection spells, which we explored in chapter four, or releasing spells. Releasing spells are a type of magick designed to help individuals let go of negative emotions, habits, or situations that no longer serve them. Such spells may be beneficial instead of using hexes or curses. These methods can help to banish negative emotions more and allow you to receive positivity from the universe.

However, if you do choose to use a hex or curse, proceed with caution and seek guidance and support from an experienced witch. It's important to understand and accept the potential consequences of such actions before proceeding.

In the event that you believe a hex has been cast upon you, these spells may provide aid in breaking its hold and shielding yourself from any harmful influence. Maintaining a sense of calmness, stability, and concentration is crucial when performing this spell.

Begin by gathering three candles and placing them in a triangular formation, with a circle of pure salt in the center. As you light the candles and sit within the circle, feel the energy of the hex swirling around you. Then, with focused intention, envision a bright white light emanating from within yourself, growing stronger and brighter until it engulfs and dispels the hex's dark energy. As you concentrate on this visualization, softly speak these words aloud:

"By the element of fire, I break this hex. Its hold is no more. It shall not bind or harm; I banish its presence with light. As these candles burn bright, so shall my spirit, Free from the darkness. In this circle of salt, protection, I find. From this moment on, I am free. The hex is broken, so let it be."

After reciting these words, visualize the curse being shattered like glass into tiny pieces and blowing away into the wind. Allow the candles to burn out completely, then bury the remnants and salt in the earth as a final act of dispelling the curse's energy.

Never forget that true power resides within yourself. With unwavering focus and belief, you have the ability to conquer any negative influence and rise above it all.

If you know the person who has hexed you, to counter the hex, use this spell. Begin by placing the mirror in front of you, reflecting your image. This will serve as a focal point for reversing the hex. Light the candle and place it on your right side.

Sprinkle a circle of salt around the mirror, creating a barrier of protection. Hold a photo of the person who hexed you over the mirror and visualize the hex's energy being reversed, flowing away from you and back to its source. Recite this incantation,

"I call on my spirit guides by your power, reverse this hex back to the sender, away it flies, No longer shall it harm."

Wrap the mirror and photo in black cloth and bury them on the earth, symbolizing the burial of the hex's influence. Allow the candle to burn out entirely as a final act of dispelling the hex's energy.

After performing this spell, remain vigilant and continue to shield yourself from negative energies by performing protection spells. Your own inner strength and resilience are powerful tools against hexes. Focus on fostering positivity and protection in your life to ward off future harm attempts.

If you come into possession of an object that has been cursed, it's essential to handle the situation with caution and care. Cursed objects can carry negative energies that may affect those who come into contact with them. Here are some steps you can take to deal with a cursed object.

Before taking any action, try to determine the nature and extent of the curse placed on the object. Pay attention to any unusual or negative feelings you experience when near the object and any strange occurrences that may occur in its presence. It is best not to touch the cursed item until you know more.

Before attempting to break or remove the curse from the object, make sure to protect yourself from its negative effects. You can do this by doing a spell to create a protective barrier around yourself.

Many have sought ways to break or remove a curse from an object throughout history. Depending on your beliefs and practices, there are various methods you can use. Some suggest submerging the object in salt water for 24 hours, utilizing its purifying properties before attempting to remove the curse. Others recommend burning specific herbs or incense, such as sage or dragon blood, which are known for their ability to remove curses and cleanse objects.

When attempting to break the curse, you may call upon your spirit guides or a deity you worship to assist you. Pay homage to them and ask for their aid in removing the curse and infusing the object with positive energy.

As you recite the spell, envision the negative energy in the object dissipating and being replaced with a pure, cleansing light. With each word spoken, feel the weight of the curse lifting and the object becoming free from its malevolent hold.

"I call upon the elements, Earth, Fire, Water, Air, and Spirit. Send your protection to shield me from harm. Release this object from its cursed state. Transform negativity into positivity. Purify and cleanse it completely."

No matter which method you ultimately decide on, it is crucial to set a clear intention and perform the spell with unwavering focus and belief that the curse will be lifted. The key to breaking or reversing a curse is to remain calm amidst the chaotic energy surrounding it, taking precautionary measures to protect yourself from any harm.

Alongside these protective measures, harness the power of positive energy and intentions as you work towards freeing yourself from the curse.

Do not falter in your patience or persistence, for with time and unwavering effort, you may be able to conquer any curse and fortify yourself against future attacks. Always remember to use magick ethically and with pure intentions, for it holds great power in its hands.

In the complex world of magick, curses, and hexes are potentially dangerous tools, each with its own distinct purpose. Hexes are often targeted and deliberate, honed to bring harm upon a specific person, while curses cast a wider net of affliction, spreading their influence more broadly. Yet, both share a common thread of using supernatural forces to achieve their dark aim.

Amidst the urge to retaliate through such methods, it's crucial to acknowledge the repercussions of such actions. Regardless of one's beliefs, the timeless concept of karma reminds us that the vibes we emit into the universe inevitably return to us. Engaging in negativity only fuels more negativity, perpetuating a cycle of pain and distress.

When faced with challenges and hardships, let the flame of your inner strength burn bright, guiding you through the darkness toward a life filled with happiness and security. Be a beacon of hope and positivity in others, bringing warmth and light to the world around you.

CHAPTER 15: THIRD EYE

The third eye, a mystical and spiritual concept, has been deeply ingrained in various traditions throughout history. In Hinduism, it is commonly linked with the Ajna chakra, also known as the sixth chakra, believed to reside between the eyebrows.

This powerful energy center is often revered as the source of intuition and insightful perception in Hindu teachings. Similarly, Buddhism also recognizes the presence of the third eye, referred to as the "inner eye" or "mind's eye," symbolizing profound wisdom and enlightenment within oneself. The third eye is Seen as a symbol of spiritual enlightenment and intuitive wisdom, it carries great significance in numerous cultures and belief systems. It is believed to open up a gateway to heightened awareness and inner understanding.

The third eye is often depicted as located on the forehead. In new-age beliefs, it is believed to be connected to abilities such as clairvoyance and heightened consciousness of awareness. Some believe that through practices like meditation, yoga, and spell casting, one can awaken or activate one's third eye, resulting in improved intuition and perception.

The third eye plays a significant role in mystical practices and occult beliefs, much like it does in other spiritual traditions. It is seen as a symbolic or metaphysical "eye" that offers glimpses into the unseen or spiritual realm.

The third eye, often depicted as a glowing orb in the center of the forehead, is believed to be a portal to higher levels of consciousness and mystical experiences. Its power is said to grant knowledge and insights beyond what can be perceived through the physical senses.

In some practices, practitioners use techniques like scrying, where they fix their gaze upon a reflective surface, such as a mirror or crystal ball, to tap into the wisdom and guidance revealed by the third eye. Divination is also commonly used, with the third eye serving as a conduit for receiving messages and visions from the spiritual realm. To those who believe in its power, the third eye holds limitless potential and serves as a link between earthly existence and divine understanding.

In order to tap into the power of the third eye, one must first awaken and engage it. This can be achieved through various methods such as meditation, spells, or visualization. Here is a basic spell to help unlock and activate your third eye.

Find a quiet and secluded place to rest your body in. Take a moment to sink into the soft cushions or grass beneath you, closing your eyes and embracing the serenity of the space around you. Inhale deeply, feeling the tension in your muscles release with each exhale. As you continue to breathe, let yourself sink deeper into relaxation.

Focus on the space between your eyebrows, known as the place where the third eye is located. Imagine a tiny orb of purple light beginning to glow in that spot, radiating warmth and calmness throughout your entire body. As you visualize this light growing brighter and expanding, feel a sense of peace and clarity wash over you. Gradually, let the light transform itself into a vivid, all-seeing eye.

When you feel ready, repeat an affirmation that resonates with you, allowing its positivity to fill your mind and spirit with renewed energy and purpose. Here is an example,

"My intuition is strong, and my inner vision is open, ready to accept what the universe wishes me to see."

Take a moment to visualize the awakening of your third eye before slowly opening your eyes. Can you feel the energy shifting and this dormant part of yourself stirring with new life? As you continue to practice, your third eye may become more active, bringing forth increased intuition, insights, and spiritual experiences.

It is essential to approach any new information or experiences with an open mind and discernment. While there is no scientific evidence for a physical third eye in humans or animals, the concept holds symbolic power, and its potential lies within ourselves. Developing intuition and practicing openness can positively affect all aspects of your life.

Engaging in mindfulness practices can also help quiet everyday negative thoughts and connect us with our inner selves for a more profound way of living.

Find a comfortable position and focus on your breathing, observing each inhale and exhale without judgment. As thoughts pop up, gently redirect your attention back to your breath. With time, this practice can cultivate a sense of inner tranquility and clarity, aiding in awakening your third eye.

As you let go of external distractions and negative thoughts, start allowing your mind to wander and concentrate on your third eye, permitting it to see beyond what is in front of you. Feel the gradual opening of your inner eye as if you are slowly opening a physical one.

Experience the warmth emanating from within your head, sensing the sensation of unlocking your third eye. When you are prepared, chant these words,

"Third eye, third eye, open wide, reveal to me what only you can see." Repeat this mantra three times, then take a deep breath and release it slowly.

Remain in this peaceful state for a few more minutes, concentrating on your third eye and any sensations or images that may arise. When you're ready to end this meditation, slowly open your physical eyes and return to the present moment. Consistent practice of this exercise can help activate your third eye and improve your intuitive abilities.

The power within the third eye should only be used for good and never for harm to others. Using your newfound vision and inner intuition, you can profoundly transform how you perceive and interact with the world around you.

As you continue to nurture and strengthen your connection to your third eye, it's essential to approach its insights with caution and an open mind.

Trust your inner voice to lead you towards greater understanding and compassion for yourself and others. Your third eye can act as a tool for self-discovery and personal development. By delving into the depths of your subconscious, you can uncover hidden truths and potential that may have been out of reach.

If you have mastered using your third eye but struggle to awaken it or feel a blockage, it could be due to negative thoughts or energy within you. Clearing your mind of negative thoughts about yourself and others will help you regain the power of your third eye.

Find a quiet place where you won't be interrupted. Close your eyes and focus on your third eye, envisioning a purple glow surrounding your head. This light will become your third eye. Repeat this spell until negative thoughts leave your mind and you can see through your third eye.

"Banish all negativity from my mind; reveal my joyful and kind self. Open my third eye, so it shall be."

Direct your focus towards dispersing negative energy and the intensifying purple glow, now centered at your third eye in the center of your forehead. As you recite your mantras, envision the eye growing brighter and more vibrant, pushing out any lingering darkness or negativity.

Once you achieve a sense of mental clarity and inner peace, take a few moments to embrace this state fully. Allow the feeling of your third eye awakening to wash over you, invigorating your senses and sharpening your intuition.

Make mindfulness, meditation, and self-reflection a regular part of your routine to maintain an open third eye and continue fostering your intuition. Incorporate activities that nourish your soul into your daily life, such as spending time in nature, expressing gratitude, and engaging in creative pursuits.

Remember that the third eye symbolizes psychic abilities and the development of wisdom, insight, and a deeper connection with yourself. The journey towards exploring the third eye is rooted in spiritual practices and represents a symbolic quest for self-awareness and enlightenment.

Allow your life experiences to guide rather than hinder you with negative thoughts. Stay open to the lessons that come your way. Remember, the third eye is about perceiving beyond the physical realm and gaining clarity within yourself—understanding your own thoughts, feelings, and true essence. Embrace this inner vision and let it lead you toward a life filled with harmony, purpose, and fulfillment.

Unlocking the power of your third eye, you can peer beyond the physical and into the depths of people's souls. With heightened sensitivity, colors swirl and flicker around each individual, revealing their true essence and innermost desires.

Auras radiate with vibrant hues of red for passion, blue for calm, and green for envy. They offer a glimpse into each person's raw and unadulterated version, a secret language only visible to those who have mastered the art of perception through the third eye.

Red: The burning intensity of passion sears through every vein, fueling a raging inferno of strength that threatens to consume all reason.

Blue: A calm facade masks an inner turmoil of deep wisdom and profound sadness, threatening to drown in an ocean of emotions.

Green: The relentless growth of healing spreads like a dangerous wildfire, fueled by a toxic jealousy that threatens to overtake all else.

Yellow: An infectious joy radiates from a sharp intellect, masking an underlying anxiety that constantly simmers beneath the surface.

Purple: A spiritual aura tinged with wild intuition creates an air of mystery and danger, tempting those who dare to unravel its secrets.

White: A shield of purity and protection shatters in the face of harsh truths, leaving raw vulnerability and exposed wounds behind.

Orange: Bursting with creativity and unbridled enthusiasm, but at risk of being consumed by the fire within, burning bridges and isolating oneself in fierce independence.

Pink: A delicate balance between love and compassion, nurturing others while risking heartache and betrayal in the name of romance.

Brown: Stagnation sets in like quicksand, drowning ambitions and dulling senses until life becomes monotonous.

Black: A void of negative energy swirls with unresolved issues and deep-seated blockages, consuming all light and hope until nothing is left but darkness.

Recite this spell to harness the power of your third eye and peer into the depths of souls. Focus on the space between your eyebrows, where your third eye lies dormant.

With intent, envision a tiny orb of vibrant purple or white light materializing in this spot. See it grow and radiate outwards, forming into a fully awakened eye that can perceive auras. Take a deep breath and recite,

"I invoke the elements of Earth, Fire, Water, Air, and Spirit. Awaken my third eye and grant me sight beyond the physical realm. With this gift, I can see the swirling colors that envelop those around me and gain a true understanding of their essence. So let it be."

As you speak these words, focus your mind on the center of your forehead. A tingling sensation may begin to radiate from this point as your third eye awakens and unlocks its full potential. This newfound ability will allow you to see beyond the surface and perceive the true intentions of those around you. You will be able to visualize their aura, revealing their inner emotions and exposing any deceptions.

It is a powerful tool, and with practice, it can provide invaluable insights into the people in your life. By practicing regularly, you can refine your abilities to perceive these subtle energies and auras more clearly.

The ability to perceive subtle energies and auras is a powerful tool that can provide invaluable insights into the people in your life. With dedicated practice, you can sharpen your skills and hone your perceptions to see these colors with greater clarity.

As you continue practicing, the colors of the auras will become more vivid and their patterns will reveal deeper meanings about those around you.

The subtle fluctuations in colors that were once barely visible will now shine brightly in your mind, guiding you toward a deeper understanding of the world around you. And through it all, you will gain a new appreciation of your third eye.

The path of unlocking the third eye is a journey that delves beyond just spiritual practices but into the depths of self-discovery and personal growth. By peeling back the layers of one's thoughts and emotions, the third eye serves as a powerful tool for profound personal enlightenment.

Allow this internal insight to lead you towards a life of increased mindfulness and understanding of your surroundings. The veil of ignorance is lifted, revealing a world full of endless possibilities and boundless understanding. Unlock your third eye and unlock your true potential.

CHAPTER 16: BE THE LIGHT

In this expansive and interconnected world, it does not matter whether one is born a Man or Woman, Gay or Straight. Your skin color, social standing, or religious beliefs hold no weight against the undeniable truth that unites us all: we are human. Our hearts beat to the same rhythm.

Our hearts ache for the same longings. No matter where we come from or what culture we belong to, we are united by the unbreakable bond of being human. Our souls share a common thread that ties us together, no matter how far apart we may seem.

Across every faith and ideology, no matter which gods or goddesses you worship or in the absence of belief, there lies a universal rule- Treat others as you wish to be treated. But I dare say, let us take this rule even further: Do unto others better than they do unto you. Let compassion and kindness guide your actions. Be a beacon of light in the ever-present darkness of our world.

A shining example of someone who embodies these principles and serves as a beautiful guiding light is the incomparable and busty Dolly Parton. Beyond being an exceptional entertainer and savvy businesswoman, Dolly has used her celebrity and wealth for the greater good for millions worldwide. Here are just a few notable examples of her philanthropic efforts:

- Giving out over 200 million books for free through her Imagination Library.

- Dolly Foundation supports various initiatives, including scholarships and financial support for local schools.

- Dolly Parton's Coat of Many Colors Children's Hospital

- Mountain Tough Recovery Team   Provided long-term financial assistance to those affected by the wildfires, including rebuilding homes and offering social services.

The examples mentioned above are only a small glimpse into the numerous charities Dolly Parton has established. Her unwavering support extends to a multitude of organizations dedicated to improving the lives of those facing hardships on this earth. Take cues from Dolly and be willing to give hope to others. When given the opportunity, spread light in someone's darkest moments and brighten their world.

- 1. Smile at a stranger. It is a simple gesture, but it can brighten someone's day.

- 2. Offer a helping hand to someone in need. This could be helping an elderly person carry their groceries, lending a hand to a coworker struggling with a task, or simply holding the door open for someone.

- 3. Volunteer your time or resources to a local charity or organization. There are countless ways to give back to your community, whether through a food bank, animal shelter, or community clean-up project.

- 4. Pay for someone's meal or coffee the next time you are in line at a restaurant or cafe. This small act of kindness can greatly impact someone's day.

- 5. Practice empathy and actively listen to others. Sometimes, all someone needs is someone to listen to them and try to understand where they are coming from without judgment.

- 6. Perform random acts of kindness, such as leaving a note of encouragement for a coworker, writing a letter to a friend you haven't seen in a while, or bringing a treat to your neighbor's door.

- 7. Share your talents and skills with others. If you are an artist, teach a free class to children in your community. If you are good at fixing things, offer to help.

- 8. Remember what other people think of you is not your business.

- 9. Making peace with the past heals all wounds.

- 10. Stop thinking so much and take action.

As you immerse yourself in the mystic realm of magick, let the Serenity Grimoire become your trusted companion and guide. With a mind open to the infinite possibilities and a heart filled with pure intentions, may you embark on a profound journey of spiritual discovery.

Embrace this path with unwavering courage and graceful determination, for it has boundless potential to guide you toward growth and enlightenment. May the pages of this grimoire be infused with the universe's energy, empowering you to unlock new levels of happiness and connection with the unseen world. Remember, through struggle, you will find strength.

True fulfillment in life comes not from material or selfish desires but from manifesting what our souls truly need. In moments of doubt or uncertainty, turn to these pages for solace and let them remind you of the limitless potential within and around you. Allow the elements - earth, air, fire, water, and spirit - to guide you and harness their energies to create positive change in the world while enriching your own life.

Follow your intuition and faith as your compass on this journey, always striving towards your north star. Remember that magick is not about control but harmonizing with the natural flow of the universe to enrich our lives and those around us.

Stay connected to nature and its elements, for they are a vital source of power. Let the spells and wisdom within these pages ignite a fire within you, unlocking your full potential. Please share your knowledge generously, remembering that true power lies in what we give, not what we keep.

Let your head be held high, and your heart pulsate with pure intentions of sound judgment, my friends of the mystical arts. Step confidently into the ethereal realm of magick, knowing that within you lies an immeasurable well of strength waiting to be tapped into.

With sheer determination and the guidance of your spirit guides, may you turn your wildest dreams into tangible realities. May each step of your journey be an endless source of awe, filled with exhilarating escapades and profound self-discovery. Become a leader in your community.

Here is a final spell to help you spread happiness. Close your eyes and recite these words with pure intent anytime you feel the world around you needs more joy:

"May happiness surround me. I seek the universe to allow me to spread love and laughter like seeds that will be planted in the hearts of others and grow with abandonment, so it shall be:"

May this spell carry give you the power to spread joy and light wherever you go. Never underestimate the impact of your actions and the gifts you possess. As you harness the power of the elements and awaken your true potential, know the future of abundance is in your hands. Use it and give it to others wisely.

Above all else, live your life freely and authentically, but always be mindful of your impact on the lives of others. Let your heart guide you, like a compass pointing towards your true north. Spread positivity and kindness wherever you go, like a flower blooming in an endless field. Leave a trail of positive light in your wake, illuminating the darkness around you.

Let your actions speak louder than words, for they are a reflection of your true soul. May they always be rooted in goodness and compassion for those around you, like a tree providing shelter to those seeking refuge. Do as you will, but bring harm to none, for we are all interconnected in this beautiful world.

This is how to truly use magick—using its power to better ourselves and the world around us. Always remember the lessons within these pages and the limitless potential of the Serenity Grimoire. Use it wisely, for with great power comes great responsibility (Think Spider-Man).

May your path be blessed with magick and wonder, my friends. And as you cast spells, may you feel the energy of nature coursing through you, like a river flowing through a canyon. Blessed Be to all who walk this path.

Happy spell casting! May every one of your spells be filled with pure intention and every ritual be bathed in love and light.

So Let it Be.

Quotes from two true white witches,

Betty White- "It's your outlook on life that counts. If you take yourself lightly and don't take yourself too seriously, pretty soon you can find the humor in our everyday lives. And sometimes it can be a lifesaver."

Stevie Nicks-"You are responsible for your own life. Don't ever let anybody make you feel that you are not in control."

ABOUT THE AUTHOR

David Cropper owns and manages Cropper Home Sales LLC., an esteemed real estate brokerage. Renowned for his unwavering reliability and trustworthiness, David has solidified his position as the go-to figure in the Fredericksburg Region for buying and selling homes. Beyond his professional pursuits, David finds fulfillment in his personal life alongside his beloved husband, Sean. Together, they share their home with a lively bunch comprising four feline familiars and a spoiled German Shepherd mix.

David W. Cropper

Inspire others to create a world where each person can find comfort in a secure place to live and share their unique stories.

www.ingramcontent.com/pod-product-compliance
Lightning Source LLC
Chambersburg PA
CBHW020422130626
46549CB00006B/2686